THE IMPACT OF TARIFF CHANGES ON ARMENIA'S FOREIGN TRADE

JULY 2021

ADB

ASIAN DEVELOPMENT BANK

© 2021 Asian Development Bank
6 ADB Avenue, Mandaluyong City, 1550 Metro Manila, Philippines
Tel +63 2 8632 4444; Fax +63 2 8636 2444
www.adb.org

Some rights reserved. Published in 2021.

ISBN 978-92-9262-146-9 (print); 978-92-9262-147-6 (electronic); 978-92-9262-148-3 (ebook)
Publication Stock No. TCS210254
DOI: http://dx.doi.org/10.22617/TCS210254

Notes:
In this publication, "$" refers to United States dollars.

On the cover: Recent changes and updates on foreign trade policies have impacts on Armenia's economy, particularly on exporting and importing products (photos by ADB).

Cover design by Editha Creus.

Contents

Tables and Figures

Acknowledgments

This publication was developed in the framework of Technical Assistance 9698-ARM: Analysis of Economic Opportunities Associated with Armenia's New Trade Regime of the Asian Development Bank (ADB). The implementation team is composed of Lilia Aleksanyan (Central and West Asia Department, ADB); Arevik Gnutzmann-Mkrtchyan (ADB consultant); Grigor Gyurjyan (Armenia Resident Mission, ADB); and Jules Hugot (Economic Research and Regional Cooperation Department, ADB). The team appreciates the assistance of Narek Ohanyan in the preparation of data and graphic inputs.

Abbreviations

BACI	Database for Analysis of International Trade
CET	common external tariff
CEPA	Comprehensive and Enhanced Partnership Agreement
CIS	Commonwealth of Independent States
EEU	Eurasian Economic Union
EU	European Union
FTA	free trade agreement
GSP	Generalised Scheme of Preferences
HS	Harmonized Commodity Description and Coding System (United Nations)
ISIC	International Standard Industrial Classification
ISO	International Organization for Standardization
MFN	most-favored nation
PRC	People's Republic of China
TRAINS	Trade Analysis Information System
UAE	United Arab Emirates
UNCTAD	United Nations Conference on Trade and Development
US	United States
WTO	World Trade Organization

Note: Trade partners are designated in graphs using the three-letter codes from the ISO 3166 standard.

I. Introduction

Armenia's trade policy changed significantly upon accessing the Eurasian Economic Union in 2015. Armenia's average most-favored nation (MFN) tariff was at 2.9% in 2014, before it joined the Eurasian Economic Union (EEU) (International Trade Centre, 2020). The EEU—consisting of Armenia, Belarus, Kazakhstan, the Kyrgyz Republic, and the Russian Federation—is also a customs union and it is therefore bounded by a common external tariff (CET). The average EEU CET was about 6% in 2015, twice higher than Armenia's pre-EEU average tariff. In addition, prior to EEU accession, the structure of Armenia's tariff policy was simple: about 64% of product lines were duty-free and most remaining tariffs were set at 10%. EEU accession has introduced a lot more complexity to this tariff structure. Upon EEU accession, Armenia received temporary exemptions for 773 of the 12,178 product lines in the CET, with a transition period spanning 2015–2022.[1]

Expected impacts of the EEU. By raising tariffs on imports from outside the EEU, trade theory suggests that EEU membership should decrease Armenia's imports from these countries and increase trade with EEU and free trade agreement (FTA) partners. EEU membership also creates opportunities for trade creation through bilateral FTAs negotiated by the EEU itself.[2] Indeed, for countries aiming at liberalizing their foreign trade, the larger EEU market is more attractive as a partner than Armenia's small economy. Beyond tariff changes, trade creation may also occur due to a reduction of nontariff barriers within the EEU. However, nontariff effects often arise from easier border crossing. These effects might be limited for Armenia, as it does not share any borders with EEU members. Nontariff effects are beyond the scope of this study.

Expected impact of the loss of GSP+ access to the European Union. Armenia is a beneficiary country of the European Union's (EU) Generalised Scheme of Preferences Plus (GSP+), which grants duty-free access to 66% of products. However, eligibility for the EU's GSP and GSP+ programs notably requires that the country is classified by the World Bank below upper-middle income level. In practice, countries remain beneficiaries until they are categorized as upper-middle income for 3 consecutive years. As the World Bank classified Armenia as an upper-middle income country based on 2017–2019 gross national income (GNI), and given the 1-year grace period, Armenia should effectively stop benefiting from the EU's GSP and GSP+ on 1 January 2022 (EU Commission, 2020).

This report identifies the industries, products, and trading partners that will be the most affected by (i) the full adoption of the EEU CET (after the transition period); (ii) tariff changes for certain years along the transition period; (iii) the loss of GSP and GSP+ access to the EU; (iv) recent and potential FTAs between the EEU on the one

---

[1] The 773 products are defined at the 10-digit level, as per the EEU's product classification. These tariff lines correspond to 492 6-digit products as per the Harmonized System (HS) classification. In addition, section V of Armenia's accession treaty specifies that raw cane sugar used for industrial processing shall be exempted from customs duties until 2025.

[2] The decision to launch negotiations is made by consensus by the Supreme Eurasian Economic Council. In any case, as a member of a customs union, Armenia can no longer enter trade agreements independently.

hand and India, Iran, the People's Republic of China (PRC), and Serbia on the other hand.[3] The report discusses overall trade and welfare impacts as well as the most affected sectors and products.[4]

The core of the report relies on a general equilibrium approach. This report estimates the response of trade and welfare to tariff changes using bilateral trade, consumption, and tariff data for 2006–2018. Trade and welfare effects are assessed using a general equilibrium model of trade rooted in the gravity literature. However, due to data limitation, the general equilibrium approach requires limiting the scope to manufacturing trade, de facto excluding key products for Armenia's foreign trade, including oil and gas (imports) and copper and molybdenum (exports).

A partial equilibrium approach is also implemented to cover a wider range of products. The trade impact is also estimated in a partial equilibrium setting. This analysis relies on elasticities of trade to tariff changes estimated on data for 1995–2018, covering 5,041 products at the HS 6-digit level.[5] These product-level elasticities are then combined with the different tariff scenarios to predict the impact of each scenario. This approach allows the inclusion of all products at a highly granular level; but it does not allow the uncovering of trade reallocation effects vis-a-vis third countries. Partial equilibrium results thus tend to exceed their general equilibrium counterparts.

The four recent and potential FTAs between the EEU and third countries would cumulatively increase Armenia's welfare (real consumption) by 1.0%. The report assesses the potential impact of (i) the EEU–India FTA that is being negotiated, (ii) a full EEU–Iran FTA, (iii) an EEU–PRC FTA that might be considered, and (iv) the EEU–Serbia FTA.[6] These scenarios use 2018 tariffs and trade data as the baseline.[7] The general equilibrium analysis shows that the four FTAs would cumulatively increase Armenia's welfare by 1.0%, which is roughly equivalent to 3 months of Armenia's average economic growth over 2010–2019 (Table 1).

An EEU–PRC FTA would provide the largest gains. Free trade with the PRC would increase Armenia's welfare by 0.7%, with an increase in imports from the PRC of $98 million and an increase in exports to the PRC of $12 million for manufactured products (general equilibrium). General equilibrium analysis further reveals that an FTA with the PRC would reduce Armenia's imports from the Russian Federation by $22 million and exports by $8 million.

A full EEU–Iran FTA would have a sizeable positive impact. A full FTA with Iran would increase Armenia's welfare by 0.3%, with Armenia's imports from Iran rising by $42 million and exports to Iran by $22 million for manufactured products (general equilibrium). Due to general equilibrium effects, Armenia's imports from the Russian Federation would decline by $10 million and exports by $2 million.

An EEU–India FTA would generate a small positive impact. An FTA with India would only increase Armenia's welfare by 0.04%. Duty-free trade would increase imports by $11 million and exports by $0.3 million. General equilibrium effects would lead to a $6 million reduction in imports from and a $2 million increase in exports to the Russian Federation.

---

[3]   The EEU–Serbia FTA was signed on 25 October 2019. The EEU–Iran interim FTA came into force on 27 October 2019. The EEU–PRC "Trade and economic cooperation agreement" came into force on 25 October 2019. It increases regulation transparency and simplifies trade procedures, but it does not include preferential tariffs.

[4]   The Harmonized System (HS) classification (1992 version) defines 21 sections (for example, "vegetable products"), 97 HS 2-digit chapters ("cereals"), 1,242 HS 4-digit headings ("rice") and 5,041 HS 6-digit subheadings ("brown rice") (UN, 2017). In this report, the term "sector" corresponds to an ad hoc aggregation of the 21 HS sections, and the term "product" corresponds to HS subheadings.

[5]   These elasticities are typically large for the products that can easily be substituted, either by imports from another country or by another product. For these products, small tariff changes result in larger trade impacts.

[6]   All scenarios assume the complete removal of tariffs, which is a critical assumption as most potential gains arise from eliminating tariffs on Armenia's exports of a small number of products currently facing high tariffs. Regarding existing agreements, the EEU–Serbia FTA specifies a limited number of exceptions, while the EEU–Iran interim agreement only includes tariff reductions for a limited range of products.

[7]   2018 is the last year for which data on trade and tariffs is available from the data on which this report relies (as of January 2021).

The FTA with Serbia is expected to generate a marginal positive impact. The FTA with Serbia is only modestly expected to increase Armenia's welfare (+0.01%), imports from Serbia (+$0.1 million) and exports to Serbia (+$0.6 million). This is not surprising as Armenia imports less than $3 million per year from Serbia and only exports copper to Serbia, where it was only facing a 1% tariff prior to the FTA.

Table 1: General Equilibrium Impact of Recent and Potential Free Trade Agreements between the Eurasian Economic Union and Third Countries

		Estimated Impact for Armenia					
	Welfare	Manufacturing Exports			Manufacturing Imports		
		$	%	%	$	%	%
Scenario	%	million	of total	of bilateral	million	of total	of bilateral
FTA with the PRC							
Total	+0.67%	+10.7	+0.55%	—	+10.8	+0.30%	—
PRC	—	+11.9	+0.61%	+40.53%	+97.6	+2.75%	+20.38%
Russian Federation	—	(8.2)	(0.42%)	(1.50%)	(22.2)	(0.63%)	(2.36%)
FTA with Iran							
Total	+0.30%	+14.0	+0.72%	—	+13.9	+0.39%	—
Iran	—	+21.9	+1.12%	+125.17%	+41.5	+1.17%	+26.01%
Russian Federation	—	(2.2)	(0.11%)	(0.40%)	(9.6)	(0.27%)	(1.02%)
FTA with India							
Total	+0.04%	+1.8	+0.09%	—	+1.8	+0.05%	—
India	—	+0.3	+0.02%	+47.60%	+11.1	+0.31%	+24.82%
Russian Federation	—	+2.0	+0.10%	+0.37%	(6.1)	(0.17%)	(0.65%)
FTA with Serbia							
Total	<+0.01%	+0.0	<+0.01%	—	+0.0	<+0.01%	—
Serbia	—	+0.1	+0.01%	+49.00%	+0.6	+0.02%	+22.38%
Russian Federation	—	(0.3)	(0.02%)	(0.05%)	+0.1	0.00%	+0.01%

( ) = negative, FTA = free trade agreement, PRC = People's Republic of China.
Source: Asian Development Bank TA-9698 team calculations.

General equilibrium impact of the EEU CET for manufacturing. Convergence to the EEU CET over 2014–2022 will increase Armenia's imports from EEU and FTA partners by $90 million (+2.6%) (Table 2). Imports from the Russian Federation are estimated to increase the most ($71 million), followed by Ukraine ($11 million), and Viet Nam ($4 million). However, Armenia's welfare is estimated to decrease by 1.6%, due to import reductions estimated at $145 million (–4.2%), particularly from the EU (–$58 million), the PRC (–$26 million), and Turkey (–$15 million).

Effect of the tariff changes that occurred in January 2021 and then will occur in January 2022, as part of the convergence to the CET. The bulk of the remaining tariff changes to converge to the CET occurred on 1 January 2021. These changes affected $730 million of Armenia's imports.[8] The general equilibrium analysis estimates that these changes will reduce imports by $8.3 million (largely from the EU, the PRC, and Turkey) and increase exports by $6.2 million (largely to the Russian Federation, Ukraine, and Viet Nam). The wave of tariff changes will occur in January 2022 and is scheduled to affect $138 million of Armenia's imports (mainly meat). Given the limited tariff changes, the estimated overall impact is negligible.

Table 2: General Equilibrium Impact of the Convergence of Armenia's Tariffs to the Eurasian Economic Union Common External Tariff

		Estimated Impact for Armenia				
	Welfare	Import diversion		Import creation		
Scenario	%	$ million	% of total	$ million	% of total	
2014–2022 tariff changes (full CET)	(1.57%)	(144.6)	(4.07%)	+90.3	2.54%	
2019–2020 tariff changes	(0.01%)	(1.1)	(0.03%)	+0.8	0.02%	
2020–2021 tariff changes	(0.11%)	(8.3)	(0.23%)	+6.2	0.17%	
2021–2022 tariff changes	(0.02%)	(1.4)	(0.04%)	+1.1	0.03%	

( ) = negative, CET = common external tariff.
Source: Asian Development Bank TA-9698 team calculations.

Impact of upcoming loss of GSP status. Armenia's loss of GSP beneficiary status for the EU will reduce Armenia's manufacturing exports to the EU by an estimated $35 million (6.3% of manufacturing exports to the EU) and welfare by 0.2%. Conversely, Armenia's exports to the Russian Federation are projected to increase by $9 million. Armenia's manufacturing exports to Germany are projected to be the most affected (–$23 million), followed by Italy (–$6 million) and France (–$2 million).

Table 3: General Equilibrium Impact of the Loss of the European Union Generalised Scheme of Preferences Plus Eligibility

		Estimated Impact for Armenia		
	Welfare	Exports		
Scenario	%	$ million	% of total	% of bilateral
Loss of eligibility	(0.13%)	(16.6)	(0.9%)	—
to the European Union	—	(34.5)	(1.8%)	(11.5%)
to the Russian Federation	—	+8.8	+0.5%	+1.6%

( ) = negative.
Note: For simplicity, the United Kindgom is included in the European Union (EU) as its withdrawal from the EU also means that it is no longer part of the EU's Generalised Sheme of Preferences Plus program.
Source: Asian Development Bank TA-9698 team calculations.

---

[8]   This analysis abstracts from the EEU–Iran interim FTA, which came into force on 27 October 2019. The scenario of a full EEU–Iran FTA is considered in section V.

II. Background

Eurasian Economic Union

The EEU is an economic union that came into force on 1 January 2015, comprising Armenia, Belarus, Kazakhstan, the Kyrgyz Republic, and the Russian Federation.[9] Economic unions are a form of deep economic integration that consists of a customs union and a common market (Figure 1). As a customs union, the EEU involves duty-free trade among members and a common external tariff. As a common market, the EEU enforces common regulation to allow the entry of products, which allows for the removal of internal customs control.[10]

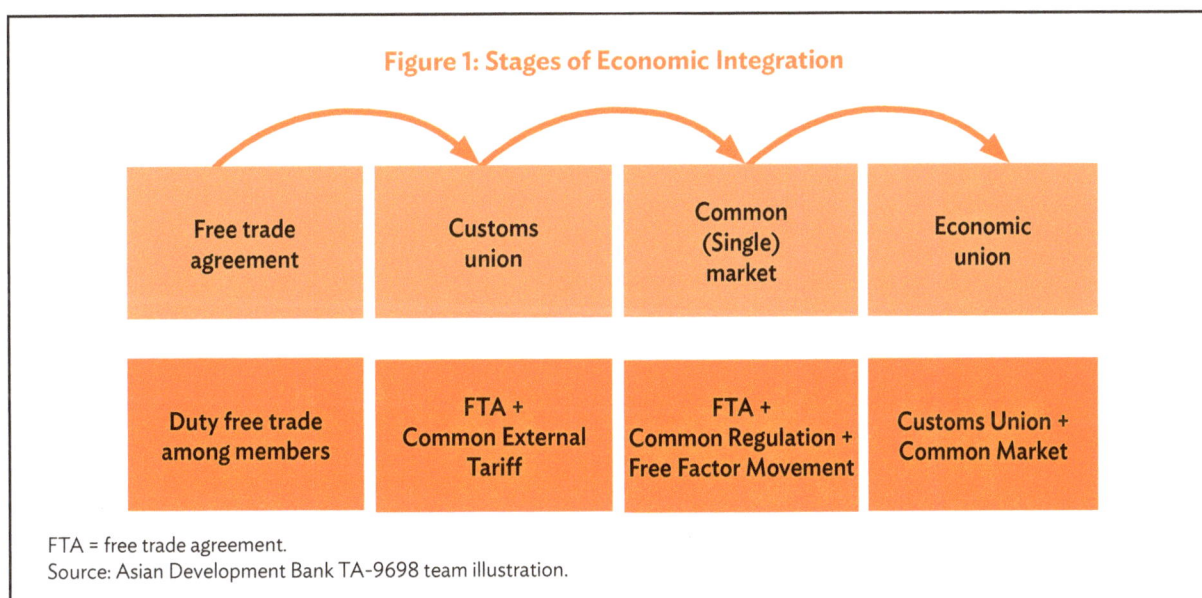

Figure 1: Stages of Economic Integration

Free trade agreement	Customs union	Common (Single) market	Economic union
Duty free trade among members	FTA + Common External Tariff	FTA + Common Regulation + Free Factor Movement	Customs Union + Common Market

FTA = free trade agreement.
Source: Asian Development Bank TA-9698 team illustration.

Existing assessments of the impact of the EEU. The EEU was created on the basis of the customs union of Belarus, Kazakhstan, and the Russian Federation, which had been in force since 2010.[11] This customs union was associated with mild tariff changes for Belarus and the Russian Federation, but significant tariff increases for Kazakhstan. In this respect, Kazakhstan's experience is thus comparable to that of Armenia and the Kyrgyz Republic when they joined the EEU. Isakova et al. (2016) analyze the early impact (2009–2010) of the customs union and find statistically significant negative effects on Kazakhstan's imports from the PRC. However, the small magnitude of the impact of the tariff increases pushes the authors to conclude that tariff barriers might be less

---

[9]   All members joined the EEU in January 2015, except the Kyrgyz Republic, which became a member in August 2015.
[10] The common external tariff distinguishes customs unions from FTAs, which only eliminate internal tariffs.
[11] See Vinokurov (2017) for a detailed overview of the EEU timeline.

important than expected and suggest that the lowering of nontariff barriers within the EEU could potentially bring net trade benefits from membership. Gnutzmann and Gnutzmann-Mkrtchyan (2019) examine the trade impact of the customs union until 2014 and isolate tariff from nontariff impacts. They find that the customs union led to a 35% increase in trade within the customs union relative to outside, of which 20% is due to tariff increases for outside partners and 15% to the lowering of nontariff barriers within the customs union. Finally, Ter-Matevosyan et al. (2017) focus on the motivations behind Armenia's membership and expected outcomes, and Bagdasarian and Pakhomov (2016) provide an overview of the World Trade Organization (WTO) obligations of Commonwealth of Independent States (CIS) countries in the context of the EEU integration process.

The share of intra-EEU trade has increased since 2014 but remains low. As of 2018, only 11% of EEU exports were bound to another EEU country, and 19% of imports came from another EEU country (Figure 2). Although its share has increased, intra-EEU trade was actually lower in 2018 ($59 billion) than in 2014 ($61 billion), reflecting the overall trade reduction following the 2014–2015 oil price slump.

The EU remains the EEU's main trade partner by a large margin. As of 2018, the EU was still the destination of 44% of EEU exports, although this share fell from 51% in 2014. The EU's share also decreased in EEU imports, from 41% in 2014 to 37% in 2018. On the other hand, the PRC has become an increasingly important trade partner, absorbing 12% of EEU exports in 2018 (8% in 2014).

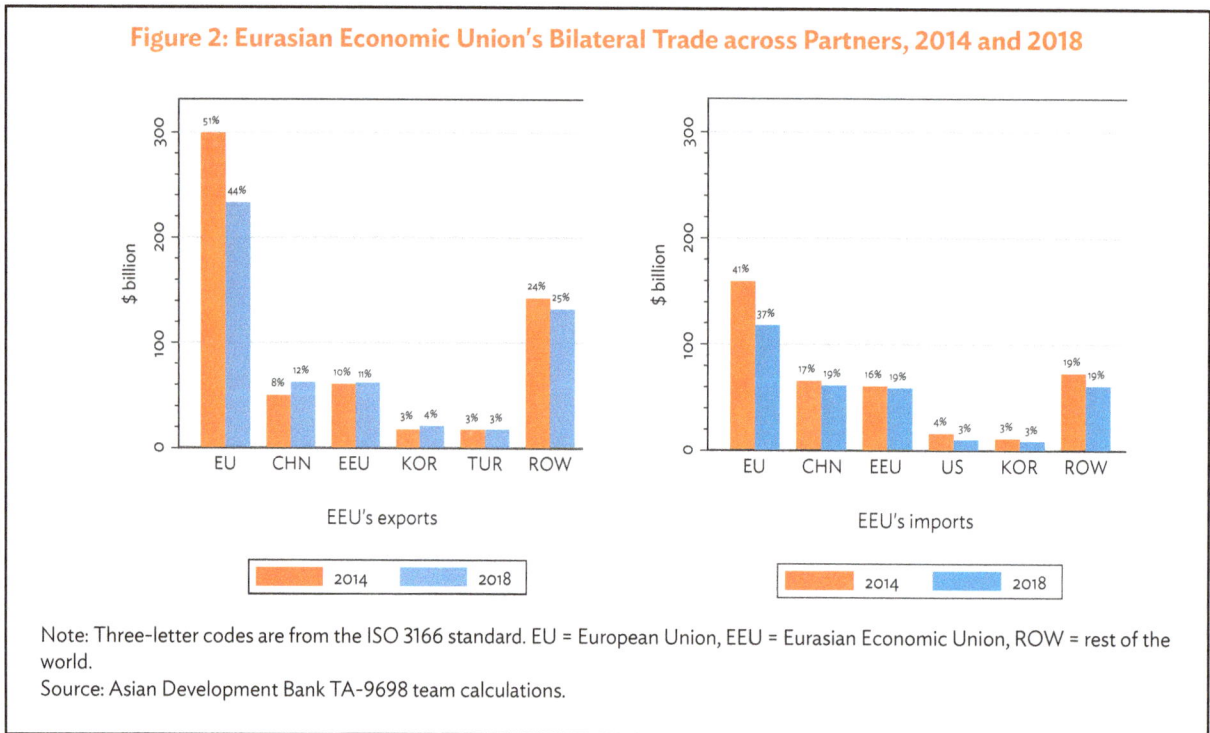

Figure 2: Eurasian Economic Union's Bilateral Trade across Partners, 2014 and 2018

Note: Three-letter codes are from the ISO 3166 standard. EU = European Union, EEU = Eurasian Economic Union, ROW = rest of the world.
Source: Asian Development Bank TA-9698 team calculations.

Common External Tariff

Upon EEU accession, Armenia received exemptions from the CET for 773 products, together with a transition schedule specifying the pace of the convergence to the CET until 2022 (footnote 1). These exemptions were justified by Armenia's liberal pre-EEU tariffs. The largest tariff changes took place in January 2015, but major changes also occurred in January 2021.[12] This convergence process was later altered by changes in the CET itself to align it with prior tariff reduction commitments made by the Russian Federation to the WTO, upon its accession in 2012.

Other Trade Policy Tools

EEU membership involves the development of common technical regulations and standardization of sanitary and phytosanitary measures. EEU provisions also include the limitation of nontariff regulation, within the internal market and with third countries (EDRC, 2014).[13]

Safeguard, antidumping, or countervailing measures on imports from third countries necessarily apply to the entire territory of the EEU. Also, antidumping and countervailing measures cannot be applied to intra-EEU trade. However, compensatory measures are still allowed, in certain situations, to counteract the negative impact of a subsidy by one member.[14]

Trade within the EEU can also be hindered by specific policies adopted by particular members. For example, Vinokurov (2017) discusses how the Russian Federation's sanctions on Ukraine affected Ukraine's trade with other EEU members, in particular by making transit through the Russian Federation difficult.[15] Vinokurov (2017) also mentions that the Russian Federation's countersanctions targeting EU exports led to systematic checks and significant delays on the Belarus–Russian Federation border. Stricter rules of origin requirements and penalties for noncompliance were implemented to resolve the issue.

---

[12]   See section 3.2.1 of WTO (2018a) for a detailed discussion of Armenia's exceptions and convergence to CET.
[13]   WTO 2018b discusses the organization of EEU institutions responsible for the common trade-related technical regulation.
[14]   A detailed discussion of the regulatory provisions on trade can be found in section 3.4 of WTO (2018b).
[15]   Since 1 July 2016, traffic by road and rail from Ukraine to Kazakhstan and the Kyrgyz Republic is not permitted to transit through the Russian Federation for certain categories of goods, not even via the Belarus–Russian Federation border.

Armenia's Other Trade Agreements

Bilateral FTAs. The EEU Treaty allows members to keep bilateral FTAs concluded before 1 January 2015 active.[16] Prior to its EEU accession, Armenia already had FTAs in place with all EEU members, either through bilateral agreements or through the CIS FTA (WTO, 2018a, 2019). Armenia also had bilateral FTAs with Georgia, Moldova, Tajikistan, Turkmenistan, and Ukraine and enjoyed duty-free trade with Uzbekistan through the CIS FTA (Table 4).[17]

GSP and GSP+ beneficiary. Armenia is a beneficiary of the GSP programs provided by Canada, Japan, Norway, Switzerland, and the United States (US); and of the EU's GSP+ program, which grants duty-free access for 66% of EU tariff lines. However, the World Bank has classified Armenia as an upper-middle income country based on its GNI for 2017–2019, and eligibility to the GSP+ program stops when a country has been classified as upper-middle income country for 3 consecutive years. Armenia should thus effectively lose its GSP+ beneficiary status in January 2022.

Comprehensive and Enhanced Partnership Agreement with the EU. Armenia and the EU signed the Comprehensive and Enhanced Partnership Agreement (CEPA) on 24 November 2017. The CEPA was fully ratified on 25 January 2021, but some chapters had been provisionally enforced since 1 June 2018. The CEPA aims to strengthen political and economic cooperation between Armenia and the EU, but it does not involve preferential tariffs, contrary to the association agreements that link the EU to Georgia, Moldova, Turkey, and Ukraine.

Table 4: Armenia's Bilateral Free Trade Agreements

Free Trade Agreements	Date of Entry into Force
Armenia – Tajikistan	20 July 1994
Armenia – Kyrgyz Republic	27 October 1995
Armenia – Moldova	21 December 1995
Armenia – Turkmenistan	7 July 1996
Armenia – Ukraine	18 December 1996
Armenia – Georgia	11 November 1998
Armenia – Kazakhstan	3 January 2002
Armenia – Belarus	28 July 2003
Commonwealth of Independent States Free Trade Agreement (including the Russian Federation and Uzbekistan)	17 October 2012

Source: Asian Development Bank (Asia Regional Integration Center).

---

[16]   Article 102 of the EEU Treaty.
[17]   On top of the five EEU members, the CIS FTA also includes Moldova, Tajikistan, Ukraine, and Uzbekistan.

Trade Agreements between the Eurasian Economic Union and Third Countries

EEU membership creates new FTA opportunities for Armenia. From the point of view of potential FTA partners, a trading bloc such as the EEU is far more attractive than a small economy like Armenia for negotiating an FTA. Further, the larger market size of the EEU naturally increases bargaining power in FTA negotiations. The EEU has had an FTA with Viet Nam since October 2016, and signed FTAs with Singapore on 1 October 2019 and with Serbia on 25 October 2019.[18] In addition, an interim agreement with Iran came into force on 27 October 2019 and will be active for 3 years, during which negotiations for an FTA will be conducted.[19] The EEU is also negotiating FTAs with Egypt, India, and Israel and has initiated preliminary discussions with Bangladesh, Cambodia, Chile, Ecuador, Jordan, the Republic of Korea, Mongolia, Peru, and Thailand.[20] Finally, the EEU and the PRC are linked by a "Framework Agreement for Trade-Economic Cooperation," although there is no negotiation for an FTA at this stage.[21]

---

[18]   See Vinokurov et al. (2017) for a summary on the FTA with Viet Nam.

[19]   This interim agreement only covers 4% of tariff lines, and most tariffs are reduced, but not eliminated. Table A3 reports the tariff impact of the trade agreements with Viet Nam, Serbia, and Iran for Armenia's top 12 export products.

[20]   Armenia serves as an informal leader in the negotiations with Egypt and is also expected to lead negotiations with Iran. See: https://www.inform.kz/en/trade-disputes-prevention-on-agenda-of-eurasian-week-in-bishkek_a3557879 .

[21]   The EEU–PRC "Trade and Economic Cooperation Agreement" came into force on 25 October 2019. It increases the transparency of regulations and simplifies trade procedures, but it does not include preferential tariffs.

III. Armenia's New Trade Regime

The average tariff almost doubled upon Armenia's EEU accession in January 2015, from 3.7% to 7.0% (orange line, Figure 3).[22] The average tariff then slightly decreased between 2015 and 2017 as the CET converged to the Russian Federation's WTO bound tariff commitments, but it has remained above 6%. At the same time, the share of duty-free tariff lines fell from 62% to 16% (blue bars), and the distribution of tariffs became much more complicated. While 99.6% of tariffs were either 0% or 10% prior to 2015, four tariff peaks (0%, 5%, 10%, and 15%) characterize the distribution of tariffs after 2015 (Figure A3) with some sectors facing small tariff increases (e.g., plastic and rubber, textiles) and others facing much larger tariff increases (e.g., arms, base metals, vehicles) (Figure 4).

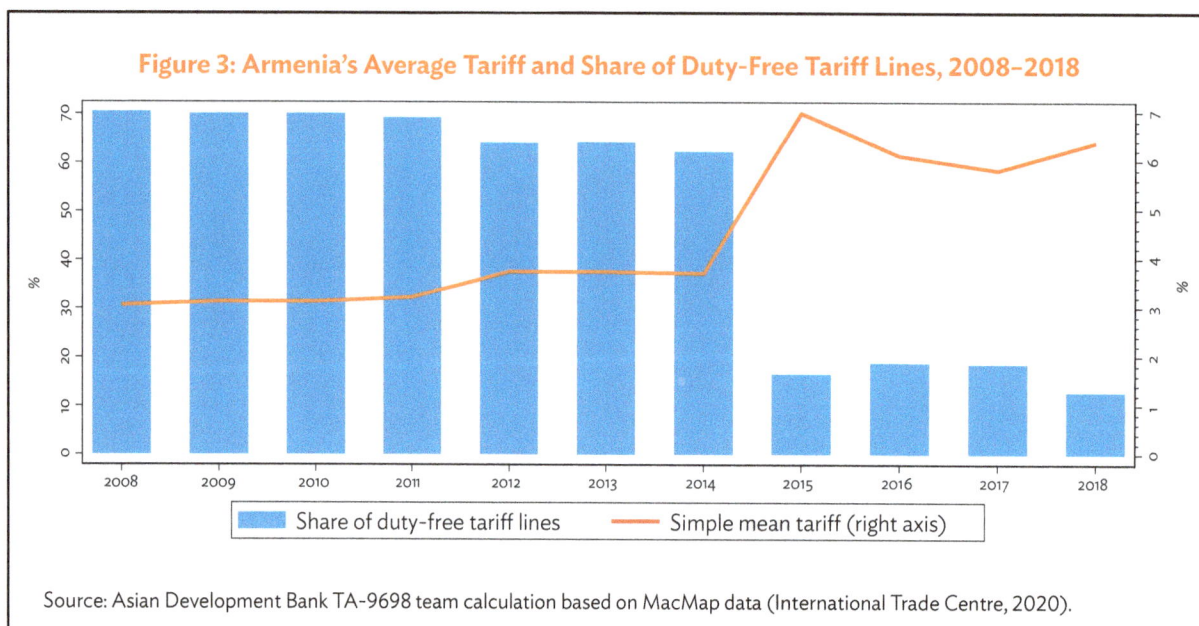

Figure 3: Armenia's Average Tariff and Share of Duty-Free Tariff Lines, 2008–2018

Share of duty-free tariff lines — Simple mean tariff (right axis)

Source: Asian Development Bank TA-9698 team calculation based on MacMap data (International Trade Centre, 2020).

---

22   Average tariffs are calculated across the products for which Armenia records imports for at least one year over 2008–2018.

Figure 4: Trade-Weighted Average Tariffs by Product Category, 2014, 2015, 2022

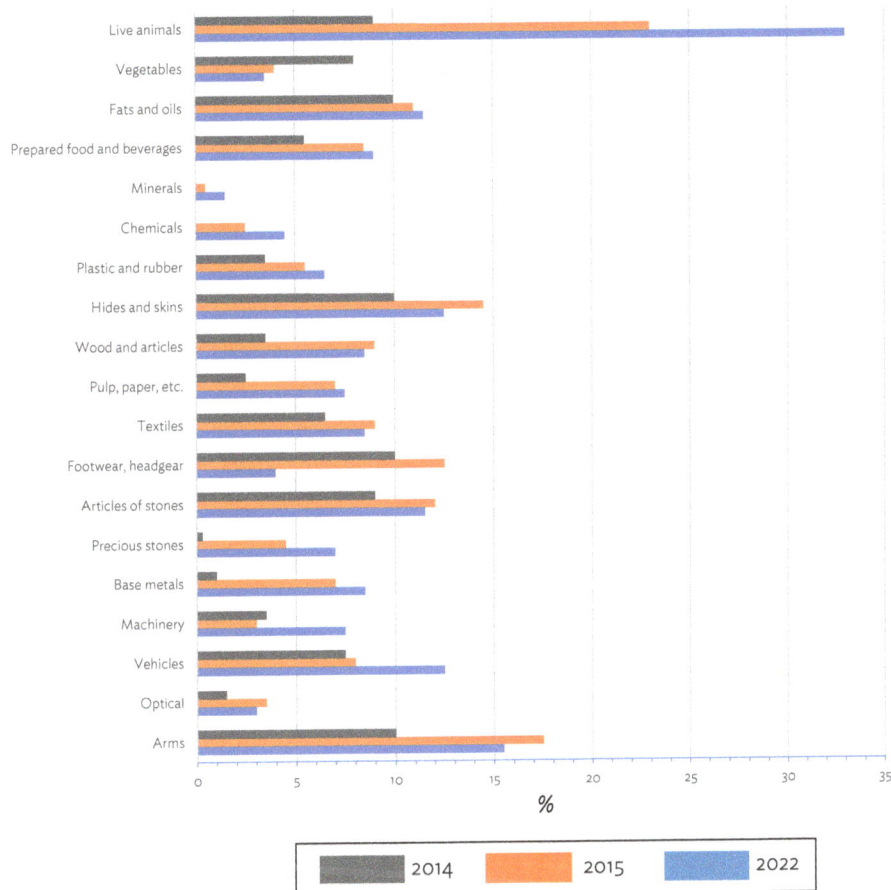

Note: Tariffs are weighted by Armenia's imports in 2014, excluding Eurasian Economic Union and free trade agreement partners.
Sources: Asian Development Bank TA-9698 team calculation based on MacMap (International Trade Centre, 2020) and Database for Analysis of International Trade (BACI) (Gaulier and Zignago, 2010).

Armenia's Exceptions from the Eurasian Economic Union Common External Tariff During the Transition

Table 5 provides an overview of tariff changes over 2020–2022 as Armenia's tariffs transition to the EEU CET.[23] Tariffs for 641 HS 10-digit products changed in January 2021, with the bulk increasing by 0–5 percentage points, but some increasing by more than 15 percentage points as well. Tariffs for another 74 products will change in January 2022, finalizing the convergence to the EEU CET.

---

[23] This schedule is as of April 2020. According to the earlier schedule (as of 1 January 2018), most tariff changes were scheduled to take place in January 2020. With the updated schedule, tariff increases for vehicles took place in 2020, while increases for other goods took place in 2021.

Table 5: Number of HS 10-Digit Products with Tariff Change, by Group of Change

Tariff Change Groups	January 2020	January 2021	January 2022
(10%) – (5%)	–	2	–
(5%) – 0%	–	13	–
0% – 5%	98	503	32
5% – 10%	45	95	5
10% – 15%	70	2	–
> 15%	22	26	41
TOTAL	**235**	**641**	**74**

( ) = negative, – = not available/not applicable, HS = Harmonized System classification (1992 version).
Source: Asian Development Bank TA-9698 team calculation based on tariff data from the Eurasian Economic Commission.

Among the 626 products for which tariffs increased in January 2021, chemicals account for the largest number of changes (183), followed by textiles (103), live animals (58) and base metals (53) (Figure 5). In January 2022, tariffs will increase for 74 products, including 63 food products. Twenty-two vegetable products will face tariff increases of between 0 and 5 percentage points, while 41 live animals will face tariff increases exceeding 15 percentage points (Figure 6).

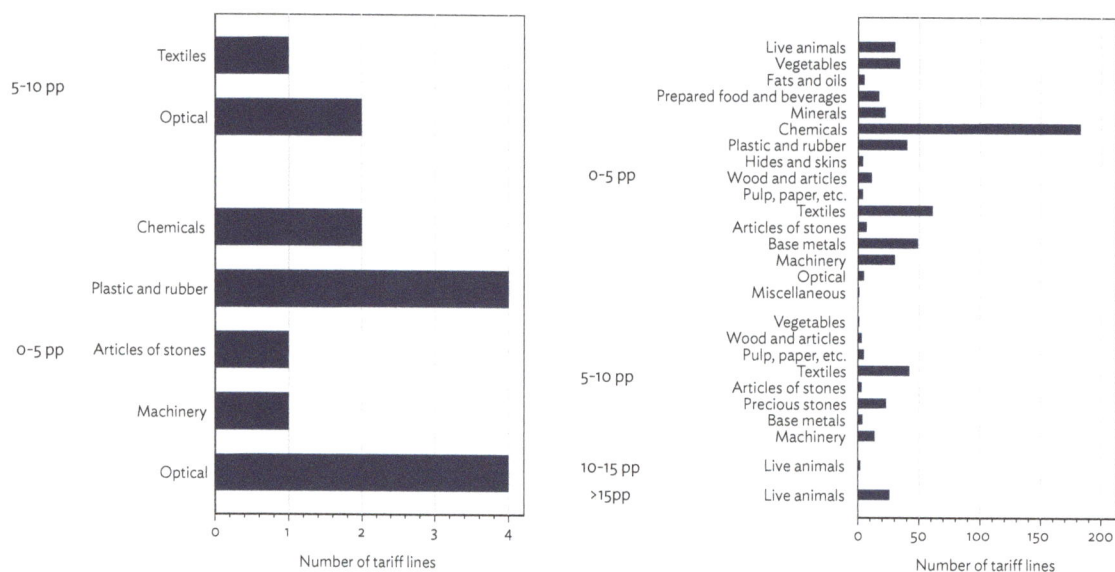

Figure 5: Number of Tariff Changes per Sector in 2021, by Tariff Change Group

pp = percentage point.
Note: Sectors are classified according to the sectors of the Harmonized System classification (1992 version).
Source: Asian Development Bank TA-9698 team calculation based on tariff data from the Eurasian Economic Commission.

Figure 6: Number of Tariff Changes per Sector in 2022, by Tariff Change Group

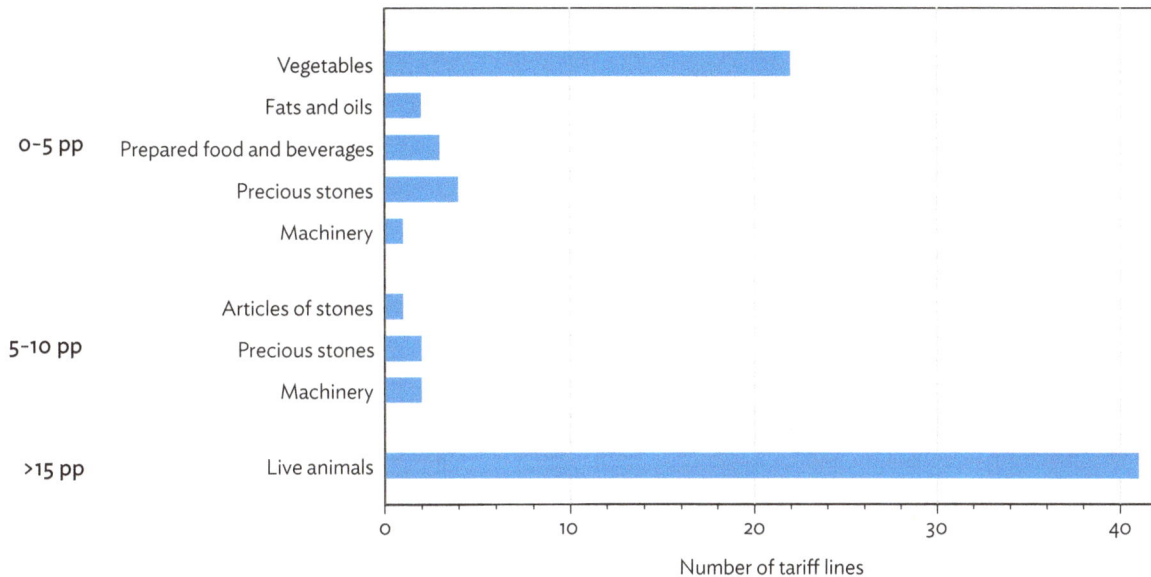

pp = percentage point.
Note: Sectors are classified according to the sectors of the Harmonized System classification (1992 version).
Source: Asian Development Bank TA-9698 team calculation based on tariff data from the Eurasian Economic Commission.

Countries and Sectors Likely to be Affected by the New Tariffs

The EU is Armenia's largest supplier to which the EEU CET applies. The impact of tariff changes across suppliers varies with the initial volume of bilateral trade. Prior to EEU accession, the EU was the main source for Armenia's imports (27%), followed by the Russian Federation (23%). However, three years after the creation of the EEU, the Russian Federation had become Armenia's main supplier, suggesting that the EEU might have had a substantial trade reallocation effect. On the other hand, the PRC has also become an increasingly important supplier for Armenia—despite the tariff increases it has faced—with its market share increasing from 7% to 10% (Figure 7).

Armenia's top suppliers are facing relatively mild tariff increases given the product composition of their exports to Armenia. The impact of tariff changes across countries also varies with the product composition of bilateral trade. For example, only 34%–46% of imports from Armenia's top four suppliers facing the EEU CET will have faced tariff increases over 2015–2022, while this is the case of 72%–84% of imports from less important suppliers such as India, Japan, or Switzerland (Figure 8).

The incidence of tariff increases for arms, precious stones, and textiles will have been the highest over 2015–2022. The impact of tariff changes across sectors varies with the importance of the sector in Armenia's imports, but also with the size of the tariff change. The impact of tariff changes will thus be particularly large for the sectors that face the largest tariff changes (e.g., arms) or that face large tariff changes and for which imports are large (e.g., precious stones and textiles) (Figure 9).[24]

---

[24] Figures A1 and A2 are the analogs of Figure 9, but for the tariff changes that occurred on 1 January 2021 and that will occur on 1 January 2022.

Figure 7: Origins of Armenia's Imports, 2014 and 2018

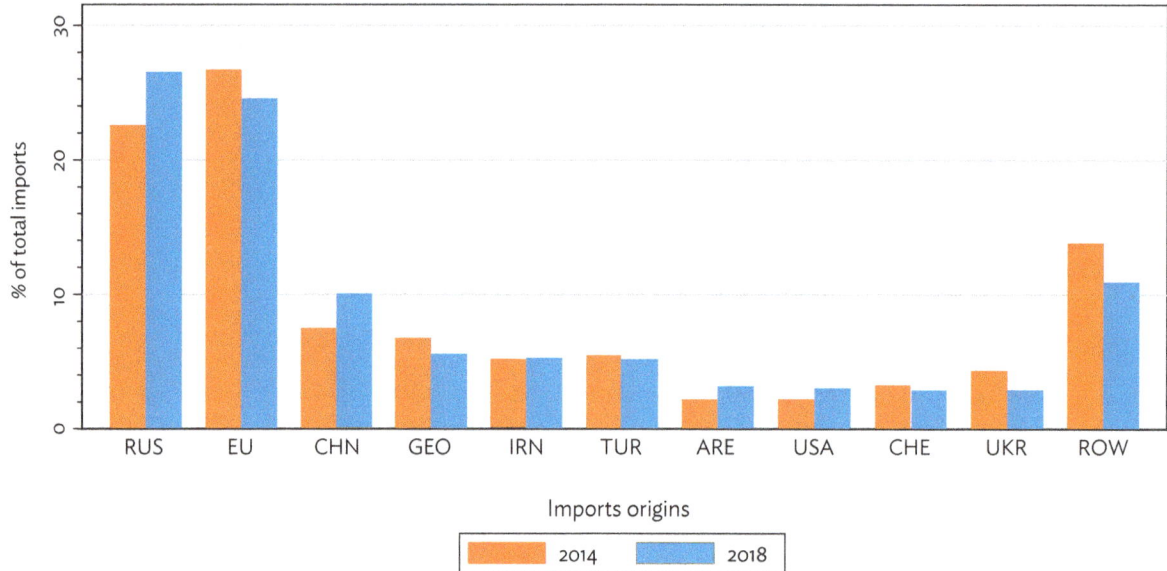

Note: Three-letter codes are from the ISO 3166 standard. ROW = rest of the world.
Source: Asian Development Bank TA-9698 team calculation based on Database for Analysis of International Trade (BACI) (Gaulier and Zignago, 2010).

Figure 8: Share of Armenia's Imports Facing Tariff Increases across Partners, 2015–2022

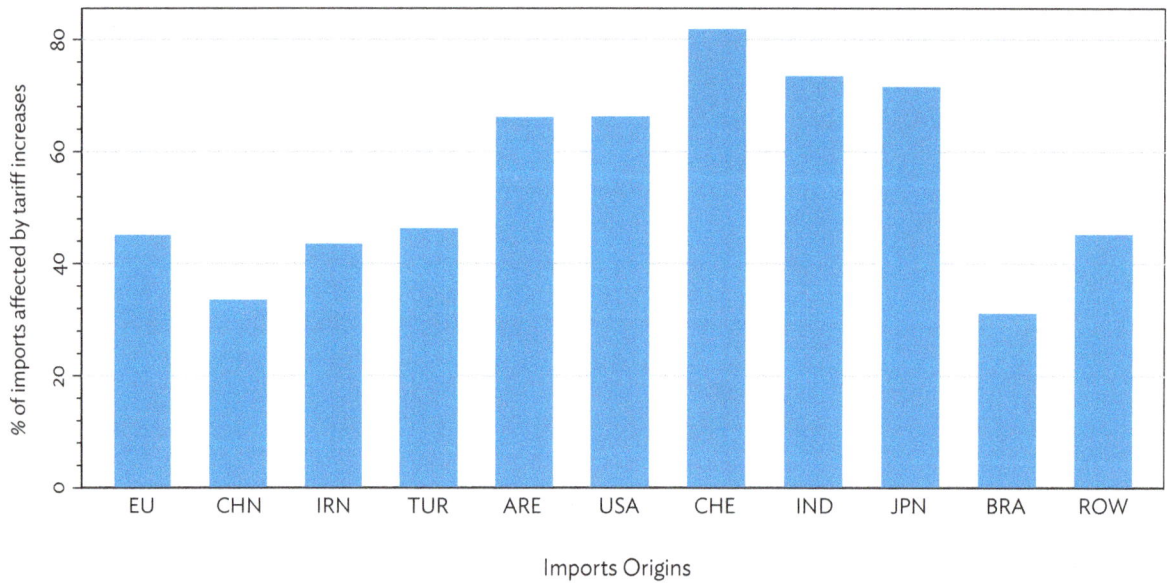

Note: Three-letter codes are from the ISO 3166 standard. Imports origins are ranked from the largest to the smallest supplier. ROW = rest of the world.
Sources: Asian Development Bank TA-9698 team calculation based on Database for Analysis of International Trade (BACI) (Gaulier and Zignago, 2010) and tariff data from the Eurasian Economic Commission.

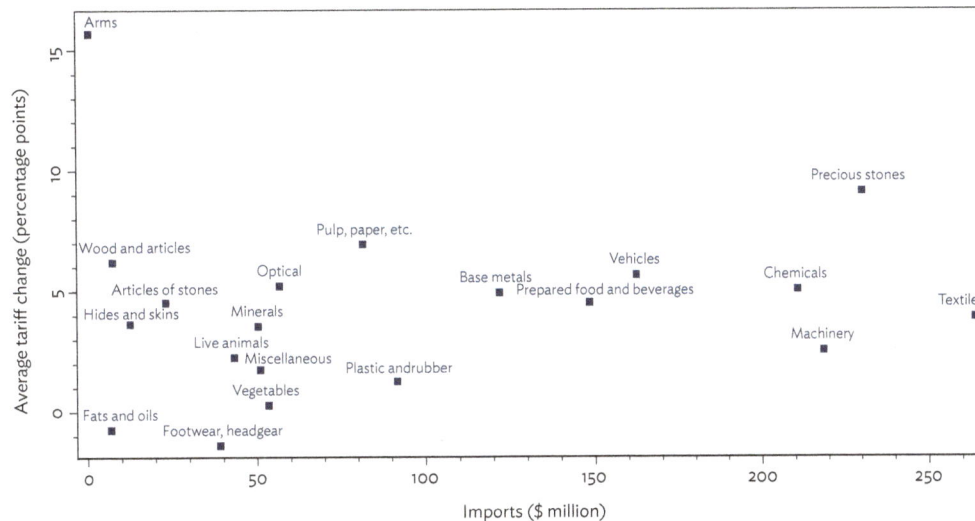

Figure 9: Armenia's Imports and Average Tariff Change Over 2014–2022, by Sector

Note: Sectors are classified according to the Harmonized System classification (1992 version).
Sources: Asian Development Bank TA-9698 team calculation based on Database for Analysis of International Trade (BACI)
(Gaulier and Zignago, 2010) and tariff data from the Eurasian Economic Commission.

Tariff Revenue Distribution in the Eurasian Economic Union

Armenia benefits from the formula then allocates EEU tariff revenues across country members. The customs duties levied by the EEU are distributed based on a formula. The shares allocated to each country are periodically revised, with the latest version allocating 1.22% of revenues to Armenia (WTO, 2018a). Table 6 shows revenues as reported by the Audit Chamber of the Republic of Armenia (row 1) and counterfactual revenues if each country were to receive tariff revenues according to its own imports (row 2). The table shows that in 2017, Armenia received about $38 million more than it would have if it had collected customs duties based on the goods actually entering Armenia. The formula is also favorable for the Kyrgyz Republic and the Russian Federation.

Table 6: Tariff Revenue under Current and Counterfactual Allocation, 2017

	Armenia $ million	Belarus $ million	Kazakhstan $ million	Kyrgyz Republic $ million	Russian Federation $ million	Total $ million
Actual tariff revenue, under the Eurasian Economic Union allocation rule	$142 1.2%	$529 4.6%	$818 7.1%	$220 1.9%	$9,891 85.3%	$11,600 100%
Tariff revenue if each country received customs duties based on its imports	$104 1.0%	$673 6.3%	$882 8.3%	$195 1.8%	$8,765 82.5%	$10,619 100%

Note: Country allocations are defined by the Supreme Eurasian Economic Council. Figures in the second row are calculated by applying tariffs from the Trade Analysis Information System (UNCTAD, 2021) to bilateral trade data from Database for Analysis of International Trade (BACI) (Gaulier and Zignago, 2010) hence the slight discrepancy between totals in the first and second row.
Sources: Audit Chamber of the Republic of Armenia and Asian Development Bank TA-9698 team calculation.

IV.   Methodology

The Gravity Model

The origins of gravity. The gravity model of trade originates in an empirical relationship that describes trade flows between two countries as proportional to the gross domestic product (GDP) of the countries and inversely proportional to the distance between them (see comprehensive review in Head and Mayer, 2014). This relationship, originally proposed by Jan Tinbergen (1962), is known as the gravity model of trade or the gravity equation, due to its similarity to Isaac Newton's equation:

$$\text{Trade}_{ij} = G \frac{GDP_i \, GDP_j}{d_{ij}{}^n}$$

Eq. 1

where G is a constant and d_{ij} is the distance between country i and country j. For simplicity, this section omits product-level subscripts, while they appear in the following section on empirical estimations. Because of its multiplicative form, the equation can easily be estimated with ordinary least squares in its log-linearized form:

$$ln(\text{Trade}_{ij}) = ln(G) + ln(GDP_i) + ln(GDP_j) - n * ln(d_{ij})$$

Eq. 2

Structural gravity. The gravity equation has been very successful to match and predict trade patterns. However, it lacked theoretical underpinnings until the early 2000s, making it unclear why it fitted the data so well. Eaton and Kortum (2002) and Anderson and van Wincoop (2003) first derived gravity equations theoretically, using two different trade models. Arkolakis et al. (2012) later demonstrated that a large class of models generate identical gravity equations. These theory-consistent (or "structural") gravity models all share the concept of multilateral resistance terms, which measure importers' and exporters' overall trade restrictiveness. Intuitively, these terms highlight that the intensity of bilateral trade is not only linked to countries' size and distance, but also to the alternative options available to them. For example, Australia and New Zealand (two peripheric countries) trade about four times more than Greece and Spain (two central countries), despite the GDPs of Australia and Spain on the one hand, and Greece and New Zealand on the other hand, being similar, as is the distance between them. The structural gravity equation is:

$$\text{Trade}_{ij} = G \frac{Y_i \, E_j}{Y} \left(\frac{t_{ij}}{\Pi_i \, P_j} \right)^{1-\sigma}$$

Eq. 3

where Trade_{ij} denotes exports from country i to country j; Y_i is country i's domestic production; and E_j is country j's aggregate expenditure. $\left(\frac{t_{ij}}{\Pi_i P_j} \right)^{1-\sigma}$ captures all trade costs that hamper trade between the two countries. The trade cost term consists of three components: t_{ij} (bilateral trade cost between i and j, such as distance, tariffs and other geographic, cultural and policy factors); Π_i (outward multilateral resistance term, measuring exporter i's market access for exports); and P_j (inward multilateral resistance term, measuring importer j's ease of access for imports).

Impact of tariff changes in structural gravity. Equation 3 shows that the impact of tariffs and other bilateral variables on bilateral trade is also linked to $1-\sigma$, which is the elasticity of bilateral trade to trade costs, referred to in the literature as the "trade elasticity" or the "tariff elasticity". This report thus first estimates these elasticities for each product, as the underlying data is at the product level.

Estimation of Tariff Elasticities

Panel estimation. An extensive literature has led to best-practice recommendations for estimating the structural gravity model (Head and Mayer, 2014; Yotov et al., 2016). Best practices include using panel data, together with the appropriate structure of fixed effects. Panel estimations require replacing importer and exporter fixed effects with importer-year and exporter-year fixed effects, to fully control for multilateral resistance terms, as well as other country characteristics that vary over time, such as GDP, population, and institutions (Olivero and Yotov, 2012).[25] Panel data also allows the inclusion of country-pair fixed effects to control for all time-invariant bilateral trade costs (e.g., geography and cultural factors). As the gravity model is separable across products, separate estimations are conducted for each 6-digit product.[26]

Poisson pseudo-maximum likelihood estimator. Best practices also include estimating the gravity equation in its multiplicative form, using the Poisson pseudo-maximum likelihood (PPML) estimator as log-linear estimations can be inconsistent (Santos Silva and Tenreyro, 2006). The PPML estimator also allows the inclusion of zero trade flows, while they disappear through log-linearization. The estimations are obtained using *ppmlhdfe*, a user-written Stata command for gravity estimations with high-dimensional fixed effects.

Estimated equation with gravity controls. The main estimations rely on the following equation, that includes variables to control for the determinants of trade highlighted in the gravity literature, besides tariffs:

$$\text{Trade}_{ijt}^k = \exp\left[\beta_0^k \times ln(1 + \text{Tariff}_{ijt}^k) + \beta_1^k \times ln(Dist_{ij}) + \beta_2^k \times \text{Conti}_{ij} + \beta_3^k \times \text{Coml}_{ij} \right. \\ \left. + \beta_4^k \times \text{Col}_{ij} + \beta_5^k \times \text{CU}_{ijt} + \pi_{it}^k + \chi_{jt}^k\right] \times \varepsilon_{ijt}^k \qquad \text{Eq. 4}$$

where superscript k designates products and subscript t designates time (years). $Dist_{ij}$ is the distance between country i and country j, Conti_{ij} is a dummy variable set to unity if i and j are contiguous, Coml_{ij} is a dummy set to unity when the countries share a common language, Col_{ij} is a dummy set to unity for country pairs that were involved in a colonial relationship as of 1945, and CU_{ijt} is a dummy set to unity when the two countries belong to a customs union. π_{it}^k and χ_{jt}^k denote exporter-year-product and importer-year-product fixed effects, respectively. The product-level tariff elasticities are β_0^k.

Estimated equation with full fixed effect structure. A more constrained equation is also estimated, where the bilateral and non-time varying factors in equation 4 (i.e., distance, contiguity, common language, and former colonial relationship) are controlled for by a set of bilateral fixed effects:

$$\text{Trade}_{ijt}^k = \exp\left[\beta_0^k \times ln(1 + \text{Tariff}_{ijt}^k) + \beta_1^k \times \text{CU}_{ijt} + \pi_{it}^k + \chi_{jt}^k + \mu_{ij}^k\right] \times \varepsilon_{ijt}^k \qquad \text{Eq. 5}$$

---

[25] This applies for yearly data. For data of any other frequency the fixed effects should reflect that frequency

[26] If the product-level elasticity estimations were not conducted separately for each product but instead in a single dataset with many products, then the correct specification implied by the structural gravity model would include importer-exporter-product, importer-product-year and exporter-product-year fixed effects, as in equations 4 and 5, considerably increasing the computing power necessary for the estimations.

where μ_{ij}^k is a set of country-pair-product fixed effects.[27] Equation 5 is closer to the theory as it fully controls for any bilateral time-invariant factor affecting trade, not only those explicitly included in equation 4. However, equation 5 requires to entirely rely on changes in tariffs *across time* to estimate β_0^k, as all time-invariant factors are absorbed by μ_{ij}^k. As a result, the estimations yield significant tariff elasticities for fewer products, limiting the conclusions that can be drawn from this analysis. This is why the core results presented in this report rely on equation 4 rather than equation 5.

Partial and General Equilibrium Estimations

Partial equilibrium estimations are obtained by combining tariff elasticities with tariff scenarios, both at the product level. In practice, partial equilibrium counterfactual trade flows are obtained by replacing actual tariffs by the tariffs in the scenario that is considered. Baseline trade flows are:

$$\text{BS Trade}_{ijt}^k = \exp\big(\beta_0^k \times ln(1 + \text{BS Tariff}_{ijt}^k) + \beta_1^k \times ln(\text{Dist}_{ij}) + \beta_2^k \times \text{Conti}_{ij} \qquad \text{Eq. 5}$$
$$+ \beta_3^k \times \text{Coml}_{ij} + \beta_4^k \times \text{Col}_{ij} + \beta_5^k \times \text{BS CU}_{ijt} + \pi_{it}^k + \chi_{jt}^k\big) \times \varepsilon_{ijt}^k$$

where BS Trade_{ijt}^k, BS Tariff_{ijt}^k and $BS\ CU_{ijt}$ are baseline bilateral trade flows, tariffs, and the customs union status dummy. Counterfactual trade flows can in turn be written as:

$$\text{CF Trade}_{ijt}^k = \exp\big(\beta_0^k \times ln(1 + \text{CF Tariff}_{ijt}^k) + \beta_1^k \times ln(Dist_{ij}) + \beta_2^k \times \text{Conti}_{ij} \qquad \text{Eq. 6}$$
$$+ \beta_3^k \times \text{Coml}_{ij} + \beta_4^k \times \text{Col}_{ij} + \beta_5^k \times CF\ \text{CU}_{ijt} + \pi_{it}^k + \chi_{jt}^k\big) \times \varepsilon_{ijt}^k$$

where the CF prefix now designates counterfactual variables. Simplifying the ratio of Eq. 6 to Eq. 5 and rearranging, counterfactual trade flows are given by:

$$\text{CF Trade}_{ijt}^k = \text{BS Trade}_{ijt}^k \times \frac{\exp\big(\beta_0^k \times ln(1 + \text{CF Tariff}_{ijt}^k) + \beta_5^k \times \text{CF CU}_{ijt}\big)}{\exp\big(\beta_0^k \times ln(1 + \text{BS Tariff}_{ijt}^k) + \beta_5^k \times \text{BS CU}_{ijt}\big)} \qquad \text{Eq. 7}$$

where all elements on the right hand side are available either in the data (BS Trade_{ijt}^k, BS Tariff_{ijt}^k and $BS\ CU_{ijt}$), from the estimations performed in the first step (β_0^k and β_5^k) or the counterfactual scenario itself (CF Tariff_{ijt}^k and $CF\ CU_{ijt}$).

General equilibrium estimations are obtained by solving for the effects of changes in tariffs in the structural gravity equation, including those channeled through the multilateral resistance terms. In practice, counterfactual trade flows are obtained by solving equation 3, following the procedure described in chapter 2 of Yotov et al. (2016) and implemented using Stata command ge_gravity (Baier et al., 2019). The procedure consists in a fixed-point algorithm that iterates on the equilibrium conditions of the model, similar to that of Head and Mayer (2014). The general equilibrium estimations are performed on aggregate manufacturing trade (i.e., without breakdown by product), using a single tariff elasticity set to −4, as it is standard in the literature (Head and Mayer, 2014; Yotov et al., 2016).

Advantages of the partial equilibrium approach. Partial equilibrium estimations only require data on bilateral trade and tariffs, while the general equilibrium approach also requires data on internal trade. In turn, computing internal trade requires data on gross domestic production, from which total exports are subtracted; and gross

---

[27]   Standard errors are clustered at the importer-exporter level in the estimations of equations 4 and 5.

domestic production data is only available—for a large number of countries—across 23 manufacturing industries. General equilibrium estimations also require a square dataset, which limits the sample to 60 countries, over 2006–2018.[28] Partial equilibrium results are thus informative on a larger set of trade partners and products, including key nonmanufacturing products for Armenia's imports (e.g., mineral fuels) and exports (e.g., copper, gold, and molybdenum ores). Contrary to their general equilibrium counterparts, partial equilibrium estimations also yield results at a highly disaggregated level (5,041 products as per the HS 6-digit classification).

Advantages of the general equilibrium approach. Beyond the direct effects of tariff changes on the trade flows to which they apply, the general equilibrium setting also allows to estimate impacts on third countries. These general equilibrium effects are channeled through adjustments in demand, output, and the multilateral resistance terms (equation 3). For example, even if Armenia's tariff on imports from Belarus remains at zero for all products, imports from Belarus might still increase through reallocation if Armenia raises its tariff barriers vis-à-vis third countries. Beyond trade impacts, the general equilibrium setting also allows to derive the welfare impacts associated with tariff changes.

Data

Bilateral trade flows. Bilateral trade flows are from the Database for Analysis of International Trade (BACI) (Gaulier and Zignago, 2010), which itself reconciles mirror trade flows from the United Nations (UN) International Trade Statistics Database (COMTRADE) database. The tariff elasticity estimations are performed using data for 1995–2018.[29] BACI reports trade flows in US dollars, at the 6-digit product level (5,041 products). As BACI only reports trade flows exceeding $1,000, missing values are assumed to be zeroes.

Bilateral applied tariffs. Data on applied tariffs come from the Trade Analysis Information System (TRAINS) of the United Nations Conference on Trade and Development (UNCTAD, 2021). TRAINS reports MFN tariffs for each destination as well as bilateral preferential tariffs. Tariffs per unit of good (specific tariffs) are converted to ad valorem equivalent using a method developed by UNCTAD.

Manufacturing production data. Production data for the general equilibrium exercise comes from the UN INDSTAT 2-digit International Standard Industrial Classification (ISIC) Rev.3 dataset. INDSTAT reports output for manufacturing sectors (ISIC codes 15–37) for 1963–2018. In the last year of our sample, output is available for 98 countries. Output data is used to compute internal consumption (or intranational trade) as a difference between output and exports.

Regional trade agreements. Data on preferential trade agreements is from Baier et al. (2014). The latest version (2017) reports the depth of bilateral trade agreements in force in all years until 2012. As the coverage of our study extends until 2018, the trade agreements in place in 2012 have been assumed to remain in place.

EEU CET. The list of exceptions from the CET during the 2015–2022 transition period covers 773 products, identified by their 10-digit national tariff lines. The data reflects the evolution of the EEU CET itself, notably to accommodate the Russian Federation's WTO tariff bound commitments. This data is from the Eurasian Economic Commission.

---

[28]   In this case, a square dataset is a dataset where bilateral trade is reported for all possible bilateral country combinations.
[29]   The year 1995 is the starting point because prior trade data for most members of the former Soviet Union are unavailable. The year 2018 is the latest year for which both tariff and trade data are available.

Gravity controls. The dummy variables for contiguity, common language (dummy equal to one if a language is spoken by at least 9% of the population in both countries), colonial relationship post-1945, as well as population-weighted distance in kilometers are all from Head et al. (2010).

WTO Tariff Commitments

Baseline sample coverage. The sample for trade elasticity estimations includes all available product-level bilateral trade flows and tariffs that pertain to a set of 100 economies.[30] Certain trade flows could not be matched with the corresponding tariff, and vice versa. However, the share of such mismatches is limited. For example, in 2018, only 0.02% of Armenia's imports and 8.5% of exports are not matched with any tariff.[31] The 100 economies with comprehensive coverage together account for 99.7% of Armenia's exports. The list of economies is in Table A4 in the appendix.

Restricted sample for general equilibrium estimations. General equilibrium estimations require a square dataset including internal trade, in addition to bilateral trade and tariffs. Further, observations for which implied internal trade is negative (possibly due to underreporting of production data) are excluded. Finally, the sample is constrained to include all EEU members as well as Armenia's potential FTA partners. The resulting sample covers manufacturing trade for 60 economies between 2006 and 2018, covering 73% for Armenia's imports and 50% of its exports.

---

[30]   For example, the data includes the trade flows and associated tariffs for exports from Costa Rica to the US, because the US is among the 100 economies (even if Costa Rica is not).

[31]   The share of mismatches among Armenia's key trading partners is also limited. Significant exceptions are Iran and Iraq in recent years, as TRAINS does not report MFN tariffs for these countries.

V. Results

Choice of baseline year. The results in this section rely on 2018 as the baseline year. This is straightforward for estimations of the impacts of FTAs and the loss of EU GSP eligibility. For estimating the full CET implementation—between 2014 and 2022—trade flows in 2014 are estimated by applying 2014 tariffs to 2018 trade data (and not using 2014 trade flows directly). For estimating the impact of 2021 and 2022 tariff changes associated with the gradual convergence to the CET, trade flows in the base year are also estimated, by applying 2020 and 2021 tariffs to 2018 trade data.

FTA scenarios assume the removal of all tariffs and quotas. In practice, FTAs imply the removal of tariffs and quotas on the vast majority of products, but not necessarily all of them. In some cases, some protection is maintained for specific products. For example, the EEU–Viet Nam FTA (not assessed in this report) excludes "spirits from distillated grape wine or marc" (i.e., brandy) from duty-free access to Viet Nam (see Annex 1, EEU and Viet Nam, 2015). Similarly, the EEU–Serbia FTA only allows duty-free entry for brandy (HS code 220820) up to 50,000 liters of pure alcohol equivalent and for cigarettes (HS code 240220) up to 2 billion units per year. Beyond these volumes, imports are subject to the MFN tariff, making this measure a "tariff-rate quota" (see Annex 1, EEU and Serbia, 2019).[32] Such limitations are of course critical for Armenia as brandy accounts for 7% of Armenia's exports and cigarettes account for 9% of exports. It is therefore key—to the extent possible—that trade negotiators ensure that all of Armenia's key export products are fully covered by future FTAs negotiated by the EEU.

FTA scenarios are assumed to be implemented immediately. In practice, FTAs generally specify a phasing-in period to remove tariffs. This period is a way for governments to ensure a smooth transition for the industries that will face increased foreign competition. For the EEU, Armenia and the Kyrgyz Republic obtained a 7-year transition period (2015–2022), while the transition period was set to 12 years (2015–2027) for the EEU–Viet Nam FTA.

Partial equilibrium estimations are limited to the products for which a negative and significant tariff elasticity could be estimated. The results in this section are limited to the products for which estimated trade elasticities are negative and significant at the 5% level.[33] The implied assumption is that for the products with non-significant elasticities, bilateral trade is not significantly sensitive to tariff changes. We discard tariff elasticities for the few products with positive and significant trade elasticities as this contradicts the theory by which consumption is inversely linked with prices.

---

[32] This limitation applies to all EEU members with the exception of the Russian Federation, which is exempted from the quota.

[33] This excludes some products for which Armenia's imports are large, notably some pharmaceuticals and precious stones.

Partial and general equilibrium estimations serve distinct but complementary purposes. The general equilibrium analysis is the only way to shed light on the impact of tariff changes on welfare and on trade with third countries. On the other hand, the partial equilibrium analysis allows to assess the trade impact of tariff changes at any level of product aggregation. Partial equilibrium results are thus more useful for negotiating the scope and pace of tariff reductions for an FTA. The partial equilibrium analysis approach also covers all products, not only manufactured ones. It may thus provide more accurate views of the overall trade impact of tariff changes, particularly when commodities account for the bulk of bilateral trade.

Impact of Eurasian Economic Union Membership

Impact of the Full EEU CET on Armenia's Welfare

The full alignment with the EEU CET is projected to decrease Armenia's welfare by 1.6%. Fully converging to the EEU CET (relative to pre-EEU tariffs) is projected to decrease Armenia's welfare (or real consumption) by 1.6% (Figure 10). The largest impact comes from the tariff changes that took place before 2020, and particularly in 2015 when the majority of Armenia's tariffs were aligned with the CET. The tariff changes that occurred in January 2021 are expected to have a further negative welfare impact of 0.1%, while the remaining tariff changes in 2022 will have a much smaller impact.

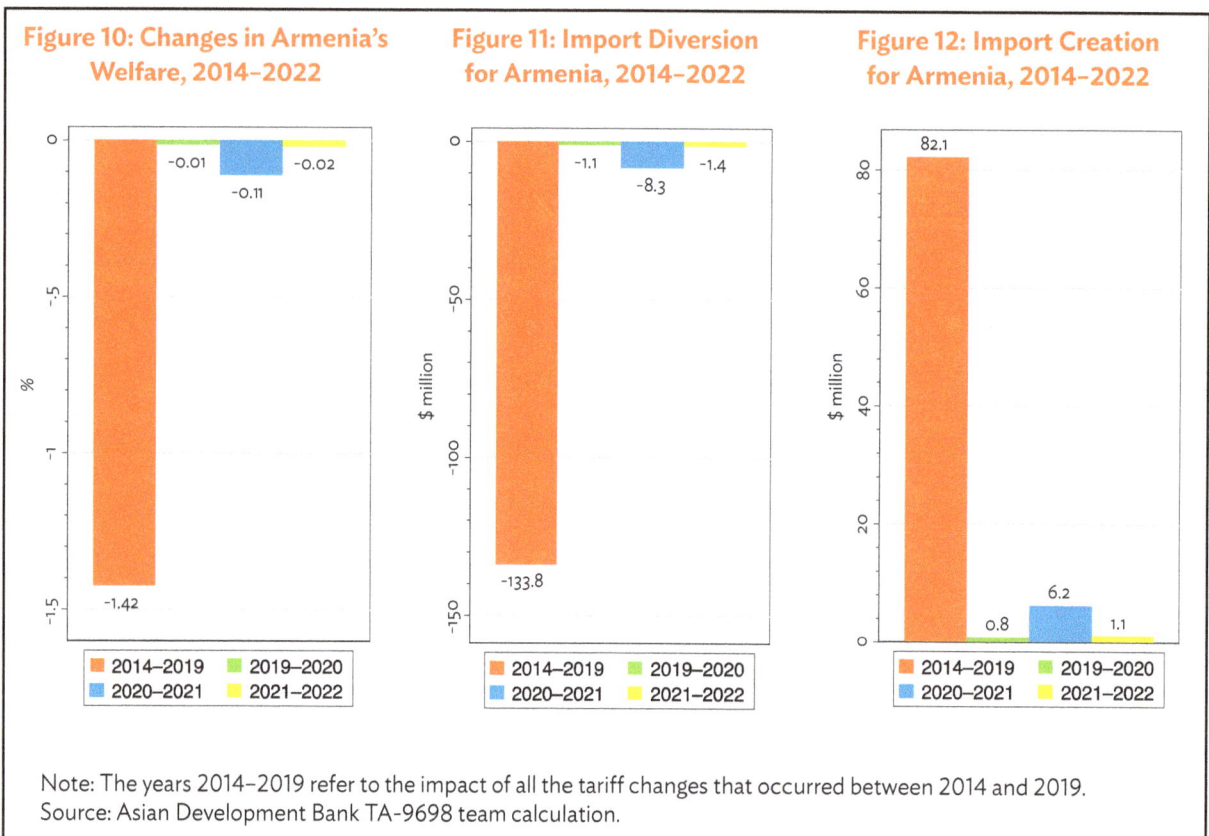

Figure 10: Changes in Armenia's Welfare, 2014–2022

Figure 11: Import Diversion for Armenia, 2014–2022

Figure 12: Import Creation for Armenia, 2014–2022

Note: The years 2014–2019 refer to the impact of all the tariff changes that occurred between 2014 and 2019.
Source: Asian Development Bank TA-9698 team calculation.

Impact of the Full EEU CET on Armenia's Imports

General Equilibrium Results

Convergence to the CET is expected to decrease net imports by $54 million. The full implementation of the EEU CET is expected to reduce imports from third countries by $145 million and increase imports from EEU and FTA partners by $90 million (Figure 11 and Figure 12). The net impact is a $54 million decline, corresponding to 1.5% of Armenia's imports of manufactured goods. Import reductions are due to the CET exceeding Armenia's pre-EEU tariffs for most products. Import increases, on the other hand, arise from the general equilibrium framework, which allows to estimate trade diversion, whereby imports from countries that face higher tariffs are partially reallocated to partners for which tariffs have remained zero, namely EEU members and FTA partners. Here, also, most of the impact occurred in 2015. The tariff changes that occurred on 1 January 2021 are expected to cause a modest $2.1 million net imports reduction, and those that will occur on 1 January 2022 are expected to cause an even smaller $0.3 million imports reduction.

Imports from the EU and the PRC are expected to decline the most. Imports from the EU are expected to fall by $58 million due to the convergence to the CET over 2014–2022, corresponding to a 6% reduction, while imports from the PRC are expected to fall by $26 million (–5%) (Figure 13 and Figure 14). In percentage terms, the Republic of Korea and Switzerland are expected to be the most affected supplier, with a reduction of exports to Armenia exceeding 7%.

Imports from the Russian Federation are expected to increase by $71 million. As Armenia's largest supplier to which the CET does not apply, the Russian Federation is expected to obtain the largest part of the trade diversion effect, resulting in an 8% increase in Armenia's bilateral imports. As another country with which Armenia trades duty-free, Ukraine is also expected to significantly increase its exports to Armenia, by $11 million (+9%).

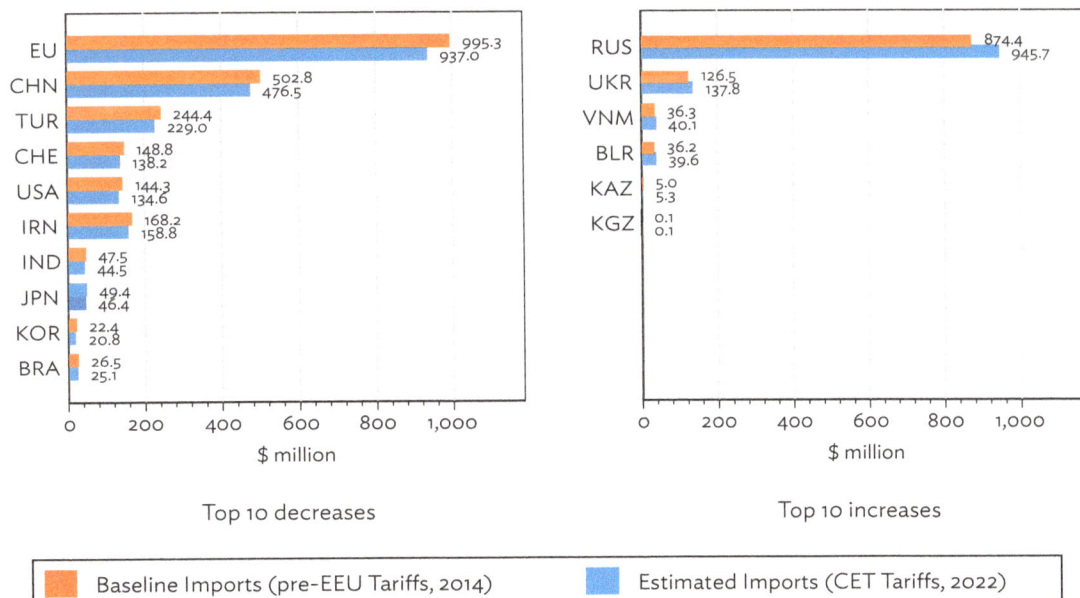

Figure 13: Impact of Full Common External Tariff Convergence on Armenia's Imports by Partner

EEU = Eurasian Economic Union, CET = common external tariff.
Note: Three-letter codes are from the ISO 3166 standard.
Source: Asian Development Bank TA-9698 team calculation.

Figure 14: Impact of Full Common External Tariff Convergence on Changes in Armenia's Imports by Partner

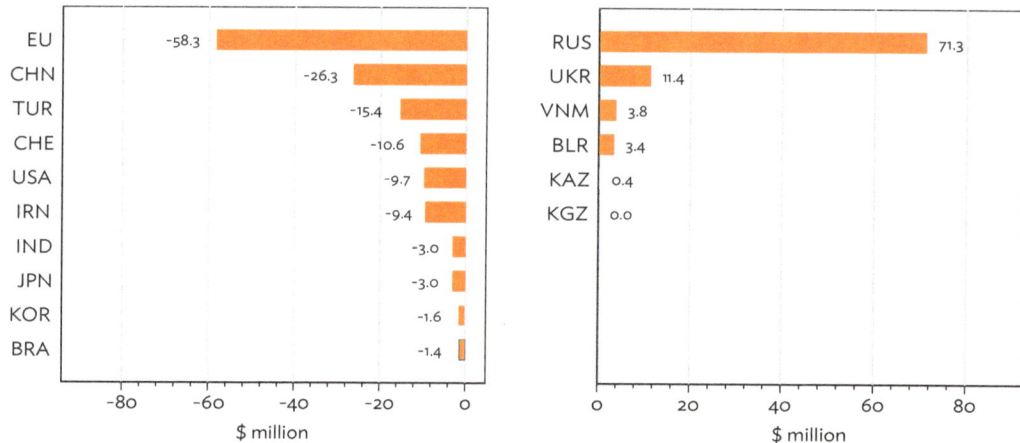

Note: Three-letter codes are from the ISO 3166 standard.
Source: Asian Development Bank TA-9698 team calculation.

Partial Equilibrium Results

The full implementation of the CET will reduce Armenia's imports by up to $592 million (–12%). For most products, the MFN tariff in 2022 will exceed the tariff in 2014. For these products, imports are expected to fall by $670 million. However, for about 20% of products, the MFN tariff in 2022 will actually be lower than in 2014, generating a $83 million increase in imports.[34] The net (partial equilibrium) impact of the full implementation of the EEU CET on Armenia's imports is thus estimated at $592 million.

The largest import decreases should affect chemicals and plastics. Chemicals and plastics imports should fall by close to $201 million (–25%) (Figure 15), with tariff increases particularly affecting imports of medicaments (–$51 million) and various plastics, largely used as containers in agribusiness (–$28 million) (Figure 16). Imports of "prefabricated buildings"—which include greenhouses—should also fall by $23 million (–30%); and imports of diesel trucks should fall by $18 million (–62%).

Imports of certain electronic products, cement, coffee, and fruits should increase. These import increases arise as tariffs on these products will be lower in 2022 than they were in 2014 (Figure 16). However, once products are aggregated within sectors, the analysis shows that imports will not increase for any of them (Figure 15).

---

[34]   This is notably due to decreases in the EEU CET resulting from the WTO commitments of the Russian Federation.

Figure 15: Impact of the Full Common External Tariff Implementation on Imports across Sectors, 2014–2022

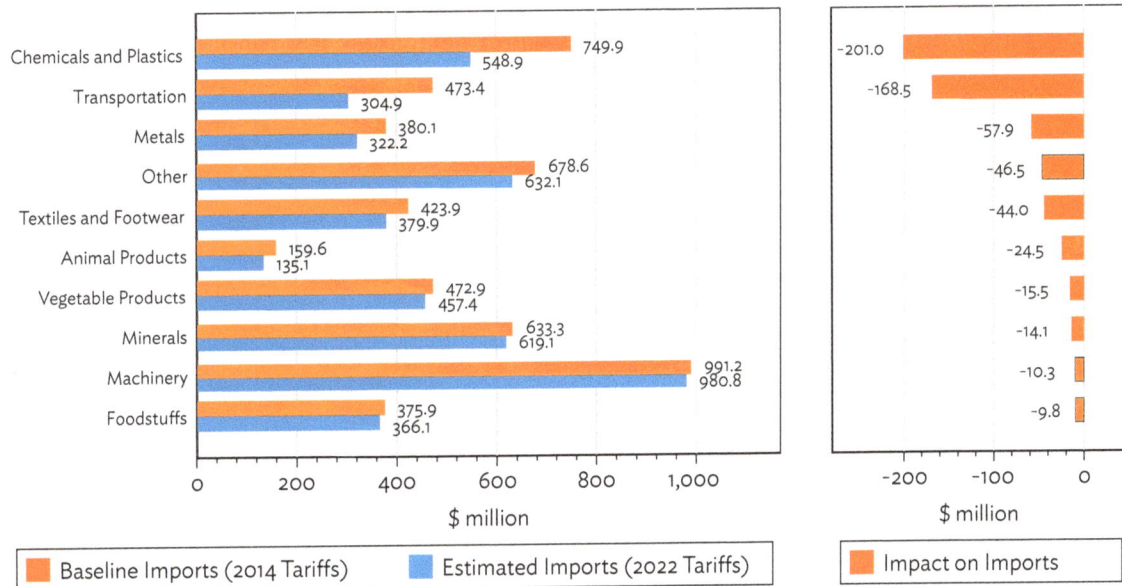

Sector	Baseline Imports (2014 Tariffs)	Estimated Imports (2022 Tariffs)	Impact on Imports
Chemicals and Plastics	749.9	548.9	−201.0
Transportation	473.4	304.9	−168.5
Metals	380.1	322.2	−57.9
Other	678.6	632.1	−46.5
Textiles and Footwear	423.9	379.9	−44.0
Animal Products	159.6	135.1	−24.5
Vegetable Products	472.9	457.4	−15.5
Minerals	633.3	619.1	−14.1
Machinery	991.2	980.8	−10.3
Foodstuffs	375.9	366.1	−9.8

Note: Partial equilibrium results. Harmonized System sectors are an ad hoc aggregation of the 21 HS sections.
Source: Asian Development Bank TA-9698 team calculation.

Figure 16: Impact of the Full Common External Tariff Implementation on Imports for the 10 Most-Affected Products, 2014–2022

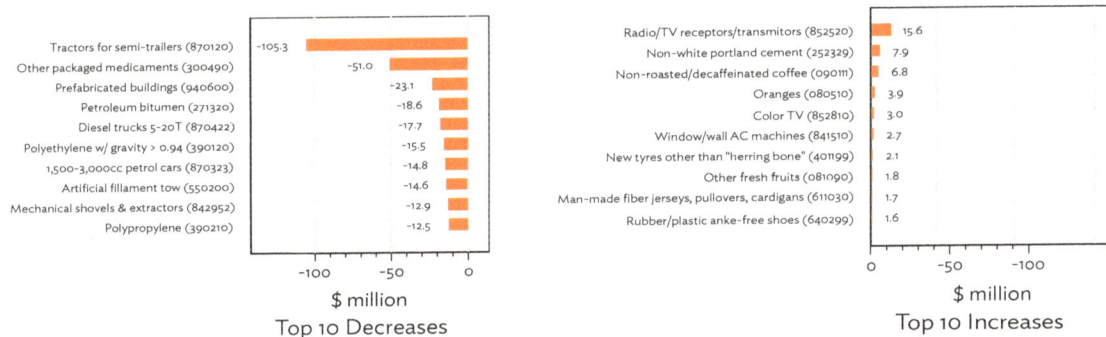

Top 10 Decreases ($ million)

Product	Impact
Tractors for semi-trailers (870120)	−105.3
Other packaged medicaments (300490)	−51.0
Prefabricated buildings (940600)	−23.1
Petroleum bitumen (271320)	−18.6
Diesel trucks 5-20T (870422)	−17.7
Polyethylene w/ gravity > 0.94 (390120)	−15.5
1,500–3,000cc petrol cars (870323)	−14.8
Artificial filament tow (550200)	−14.6
Mechanical shovels & extractors (842952)	−12.9
Polypropylene (390210)	−12.5

Top 10 Increases ($ million)

Product	Impact
Radio/TV receptors/transmitors (852520)	15.6
Non-white portland cement (252329)	7.9
Non-roasted/decaffeinated coffee (090111)	6.8
Oranges (080510)	3.9
Color TV (852810)	3.0
Window/wall AC machines (841510)	2.7
New tyres other than "herring bone" (401199)	2.1
Other fresh fruits (081090)	1.8
Man-made fiber jerseys, pullovers, cardigans (611030)	1.7
Rubber/plastic anke-free shoes (640299)	1.6

Note: Partial equilibrium results. Numbers in parentheses correspond to 6-digit product codes in the Harmonized System classification (1992 version).
Source: Asian Development Bank TA-9698 team calculation.

Impact of 2021 and 2022 Tariff Changes on Armenia's Imports

General Equilibrium Results

The tariff changes that occurred in January 2021 should have a limited impact.[35] The tariff changes that occurred in January 2021 are expected to reduce imports of manufactured goods by $8 million, mostly from the EU (–$3.4 million) and the PRC (–$1.7 million) (Figure 17). On the other hand, trade reallocation is expected to increase imports by $6 million, mostly from the Russian Federation (+$5 million). Overall, these changes are expected to reduce Armenia's imports by $2 million (–0.06%) (Figure 17). The overall impact was limited as tariffs increased for 626 products only in January 2021. However, the impact might still be sizeable in the sectors where the tariff increases concentrate, including precious stones, live animals, textiles, and chemicals (e.g., pharmaceuticals) (Figure 5).

The tariff changes that will occur in January 2022 should have an even smaller impact. The tariff changes that will occur in January 2022 are expected to reduce net imports by less than $300,000 (Figure 18).

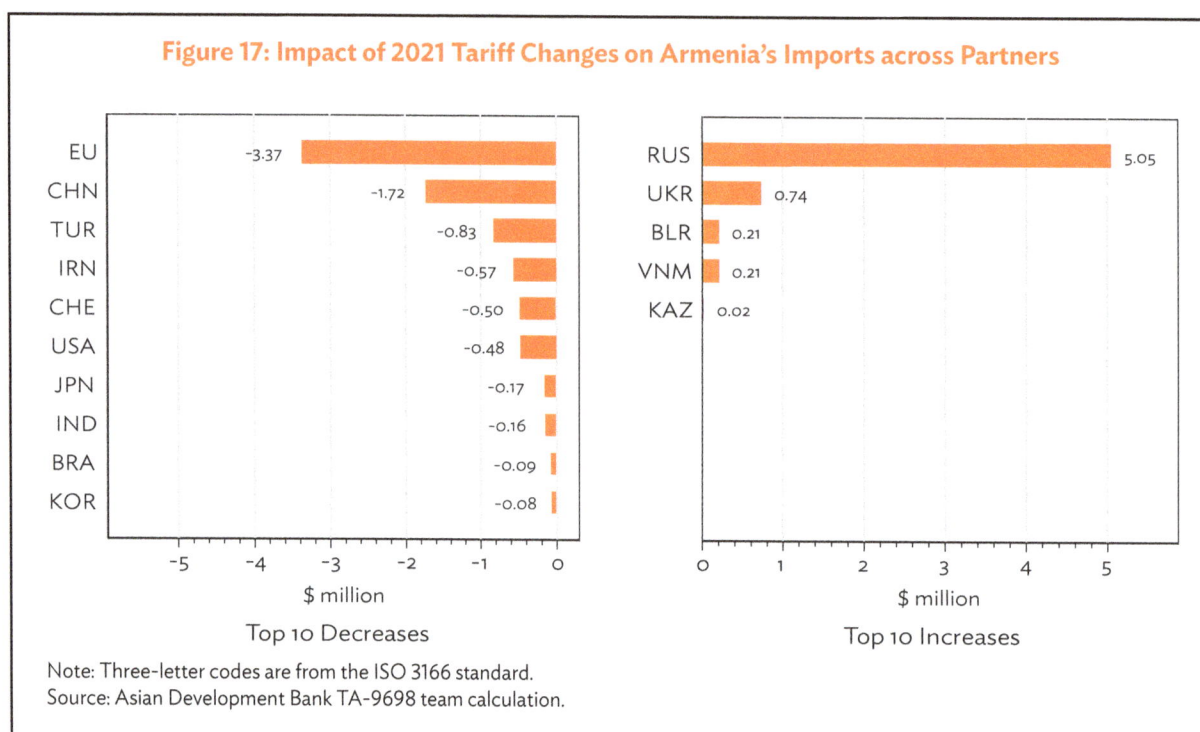

Figure 17: Impact of 2021 Tariff Changes on Armenia's Imports across Partners

Top 10 Decreases

	$ million
EU	-3.37
CHN	-1.72
TUR	-0.83
IRN	-0.57
CHE	-0.50
USA	-0.48
JPN	-0.17
IND	-0.16
BRA	-0.09
KOR	-0.08

Top 10 Increases

	$ million
RUS	5.05
UKR	0.74
BLR	0.21
VNM	0.21
KAZ	0.02

Note: Three-letter codes are from the ISO 3166 standard.
Source: Asian Development Bank TA-9698 team calculation.

[35]   This section discusses tariff changes that occurred on 1 January 2021 and that will occur on 1 January 2022. The tariff changes that occurred on 1 January in 2020 are estimated to have reduced Armenia's vehicles imports by about $48 million, including petrol cars (–$25 million) and diesel trucks (–$12 million).

Figure 18: Impact of 2022 Tariff Changes on Armenia's Imports across Partners

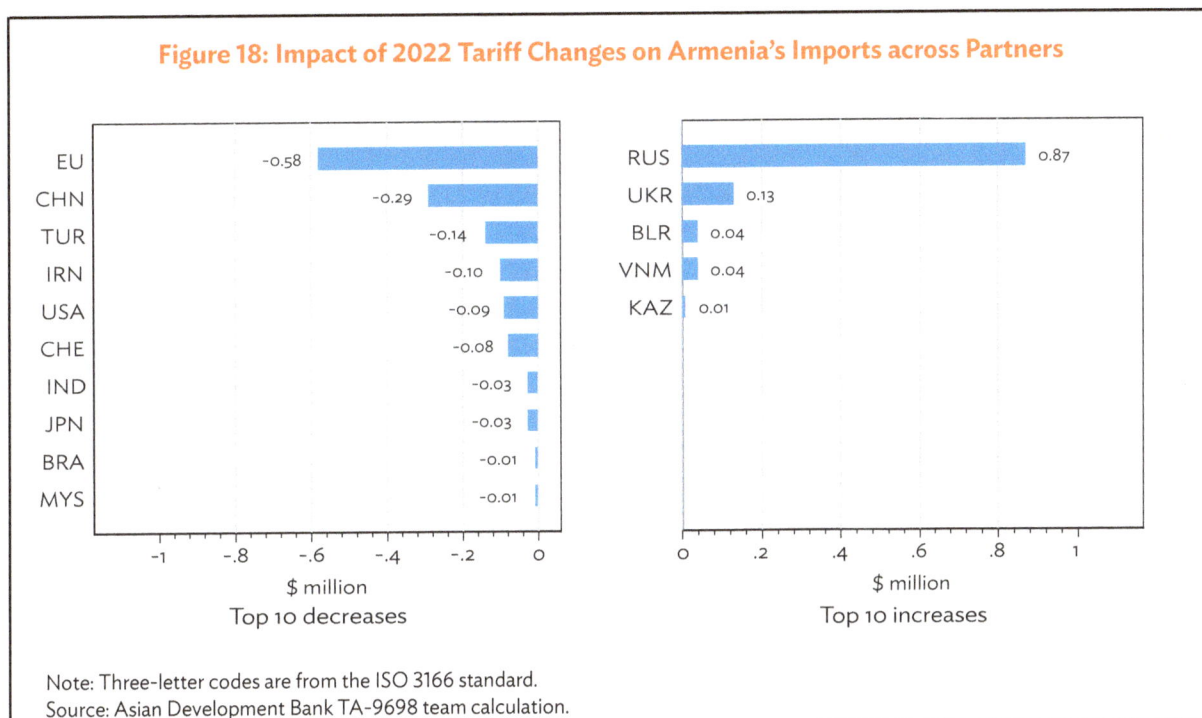

Top 10 decreases:
- EU −0.58
- CHN −0.29
- TUR −0.14
- IRN −0.10
- USA −0.09
- CHE −0.08
- IND −0.03
- JPN −0.03
- BRA −0.01
- MYS −0.01

$ million — Top 10 decreases

Top 10 increases:
- RUS 0.87
- UKR 0.13
- BLR 0.04
- VNM 0.04
- KAZ 0.01

$ million — Top 10 increases

Note: Three-letter codes are from the ISO 3166 standard.
Source: Asian Development Bank TA-9698 team calculation.

Partial Equilibrium Results

The tariff increases that took effect on 1 January 2021 could reduce imports by up to $111 million.[36] Import reductions should concentrate in chemicals and plastics (−$55 million), particularly affecting medicaments (−$30 million), but also specific plastics such as polypropylene (−$7 million) and polyethylene (−$2 million) (Figures 19 and 20). Imports of petroleum bitumen (i.e., asphalt) should also decline by $9 million.

The tariff increase that will take place on 1 January 2022 should only reduce imports by $14 million. The impact is expected to concentrate almost entirely on frozen pork (Figures 21 and 22).

---

[36] The impacts of tariff changes on 1 January 2021 and 1 January 2022 are included in the impact of the full implementation of the CET, detailed in the section discussing the impact of the full EEU CET on Armenia's imports.

Figure 19: Impact of 2021 Tariff Changes on Armenia's Imports across Sectors

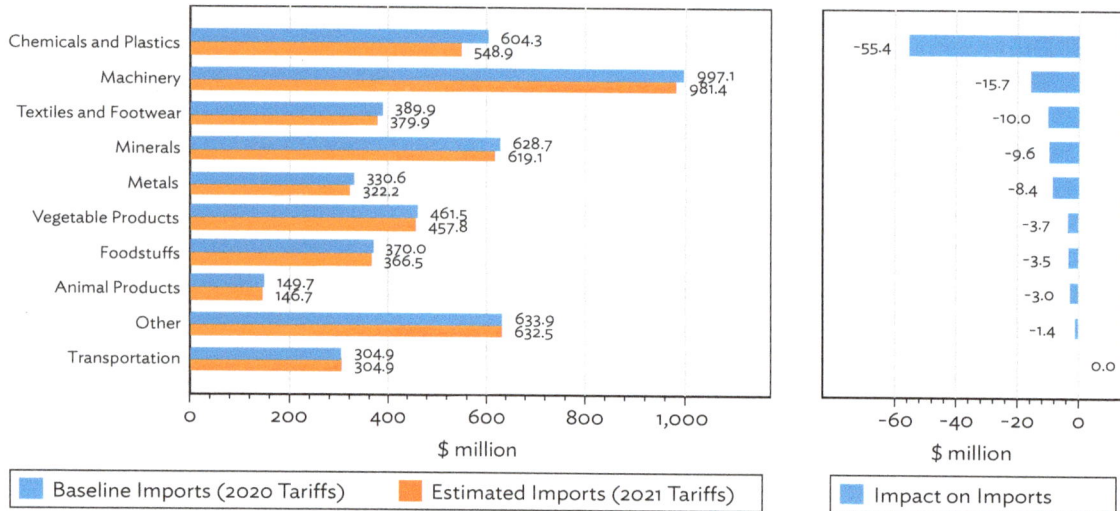

Sector	Baseline Imports (2020 Tariffs)	Estimated Imports (2021 Tariffs)	Impact on Imports
Chemicals and Plastics	604.3	548.9	-55.4
Machinery	997.1	981.4	-15.7
Textiles and Footwear	389.9	379.9	-10.0
Minerals	628.7	619.1	-9.6
Metals	330.6	322.2	-8.4
Vegetable Products	461.5	457.8	-3.7
Foodstuffs	370.0	366.5	-3.5
Animal Products	149.7	146.7	-3.0
Other	633.9	632.5	-1.4
Transportation	304.9	304.9	0.0

$ million

■ Baseline Imports (2020 Tariffs)   ■ Estimated Imports (2021 Tariffs)   ■ Impact on Imports

Note: Partial equilibrium results. Harmonized System (HS) sectors are an ad-hoc aggregation of the 21 HS sections.
Source: Asian Development Bank TA-9698 team calculation.

Figure 20: Impact of 2021 Tariff Changes on Armenia's Imports for the 10 Most-Affected Products

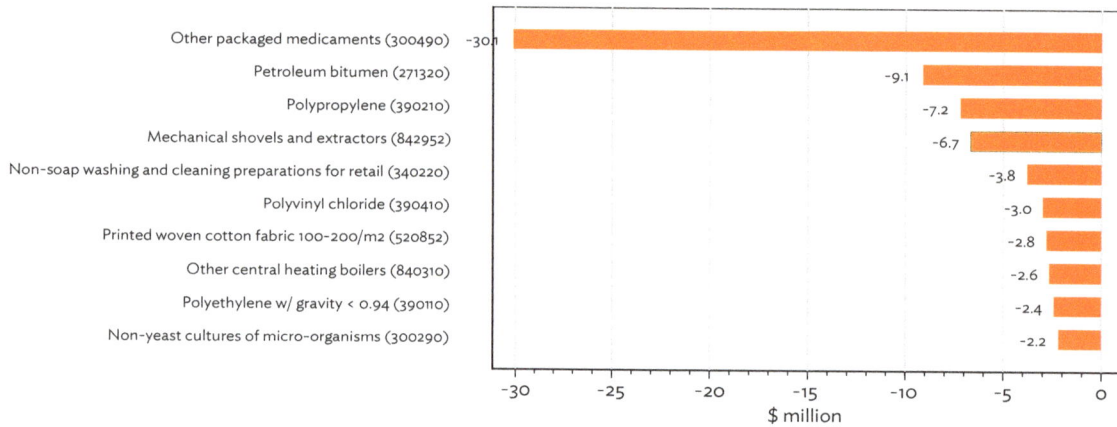

Product	Impact ($ million)
Other packaged medicaments (300490)	-30.1
Petroleum bitumen (271320)	-9.1
Polypropylene (390210)	-7.2
Mechanical shovels and extractors (842952)	-6.7
Non-soap washing and cleaning preparations for retail (340220)	-3.8
Polyvinyl chloride (390410)	-3.0
Printed woven cotton fabric 100-200/m2 (520852)	-2.8
Other central heating boilers (840310)	-2.6
Polyethylene w/ gravity < 0.94 (390110)	-2.4
Non-yeast cultures of micro-organisms (300290)	-2.2

$ million

Note: Partial equilibrium results. Numbers in parentheses correspond to 6-digit product codes in the Harmonized System classification (1992 version).
Source: Asian Development Bank TA-9698 team calculation.

Figure 21: Impact of 2022 Tariff Changes on Armenia's Imports across Sectors

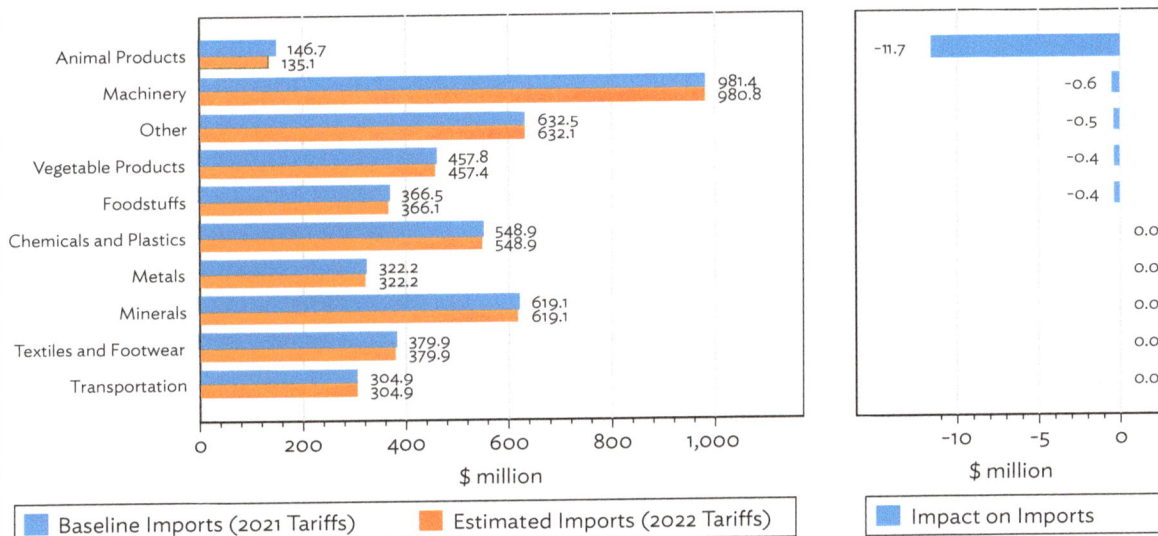

	Baseline Imports (2021 Tariffs)	Estimated Imports (2022 Tariffs)	Impact on Imports
Animal Products	146.7	135.1	−11.7
Machinery	981.4	980.8	−0.6
Other	632.5	632.1	−0.5
Vegetable Products	457.8	457.4	−0.4
Foodstuffs	366.5	366.1	−0.4
Chemicals and Plastics	548.9	548.9	0.0
Metals	322.2	322.2	0.0
Minerals	619.1	619.1	0.0
Textiles and Footwear	379.9	379.9	0.0
Transportation	304.9	304.9	0.0

Note: Partial equilibrium results. Harmonized System (HS) sectors are an ad-hoc aggregation of the 21 HS sections.
Source: Asian Development Bank TA-9698 team calculation.

Figure 22: Impact of 2022 Tariff Changes on Armenia's Imports for the 10 Most-Affected Products

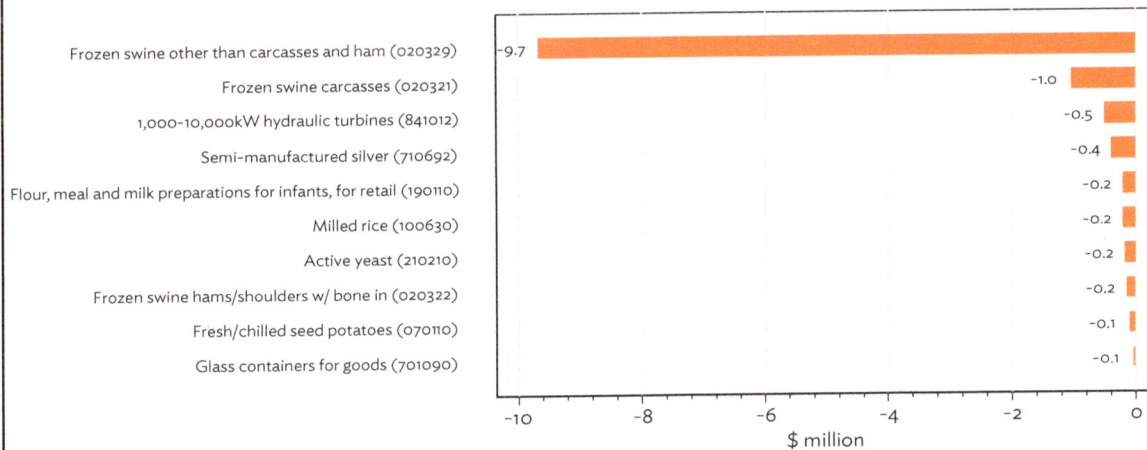

Product	$ million
Frozen swine other than carcasses and ham (020329)	−9.7
Frozen swine carcasses (020321)	−1.0
1,000–10,000kW hydraulic turbines (841012)	−0.5
Semi-manufactured silver (710692)	−0.4
Flour, meal and milk preparations for infants, for retail (190110)	−0.2
Milled rice (100630)	−0.2
Active yeast (210210)	−0.2
Frozen swine hams/shoulders w/ bone in (020322)	−0.2
Fresh/chilled seed potatoes (070110)	−0.1
Glass containers for goods (701090)	−0.1

Note: Partial equilibrium results. Numbers in parentheses correspond to 6-digit product codes in the Harmonized System classification (1992 version).
Source: Asian Development Bank TA-9698 team calculation.

Impact of a Potential Free Trade Agreement with India

An EEU–India FTA could be signed in 2021. The EEU has been negotiating an FTA with India since June 2015 (ADB, 2020). Negotiations were revived in January 2020 as the foreign minister of the Russian Federation visited India, with the objective of concluding negotiations by the end of 2020 (Simes, 2020). The conclusion of the Regional Comprehensive Economic Partnership in November 2020—that India eventually did not sign—might also free resources to conclude the EEU–India FTA in 2021.

Armenia sources 1.3% of its imports from India, but its exports to India are minuscule. Armenia imported $62 million from India in 2018 but exported less than $1 million (Figure 23). Imports are largely composed of raw tobacco (26%), which is processed into cigarettes in Armenia before being re-exported to Iraq, Syria, and the United Arab Emirates (UAE). Diamonds also account for 23% of Armenia's imports from India. Here again, diamonds are processed into jewelry, which are then largely exported, notably to the UAE and the former Soviet Union.

General equilibrium: An EEU–India FTA would have a modest impact on Armenia's welfare and manufacturing trade. The general equilibrium analysis shows that an FTA with India would increase Armenia's and India's welfare by 0.04%. Among EEU partners, Belarus would reap the largest benefits (0.07%), followed by the Russian Federation (0.05%) (Figure 24).[37] Armenia's manufacturing exports to India would not significantly increase ($0.3 million) under an FTA. The modest impact is caused by small preexisting bilateral exports to India of less than $1 million (Figure 23). Armenia's manufactured imports from India would increase by $11 million, making up about 20% of bilateral imports.

Partial equilibrium: An EEU–India FTA would mostly increase Armenia's imports of plastics, medicaments, electrical equipment, and raw tobacco from India. The partial equilibrium analysis confirms the magnitude of the impact, with the elimination of tariffs increasing Armenia's imports from India by $14 million ($11 million in general equilibrium), and only marginally affecting Armenia's exports (Figure 25 and Figure 26). The largest impact on imports would be for chemicals and plastics (+$6.1 million), including polyethylene terephthalate (PET, a plastic notably used in containers for liquids and foods, +$3.0 million) and packaged medicaments (+$1.9 million). Imports of machinery would also increase by $3.0 million, notably high-voltage protection equipment (+$1.5 million) and electrical insulators (+$0.6 million). An FTA would also increase Armenia's imports of raw tobacco (+$1.4 million). Finally, the limited impact on Armenia's exports would concentrate on radio and TV receptors and monumental and building stones (+$0.1 million each).

---

[37]   This is linked to the intensity of existing trade between Belarus and India and the current level of tariffs. Belarus exported $309 million to India in 2018, including $250 million of potassic fertilizers, accounting for close to a quarter of India's supply. Potassic fertilizers, in turn, face a 7.5% tariff when imported to India. India exported $125 million to Belarus in 2018, including $30 million of pharmaceutical products, which face a 10% tariff when imported into the EEU.

Figure 23: Sectoral Composition of Armenia–India Trade, 2008–2018

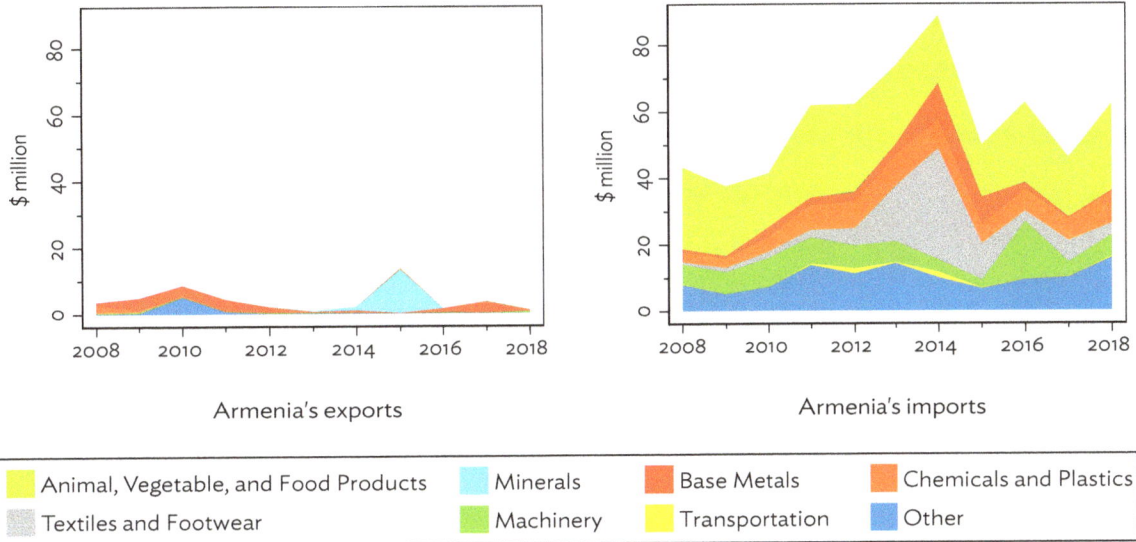

Armenia's exports

Armenia's imports

Legend:
- Animal, Vegetable, and Food Products
- Minerals
- Base Metals
- Chemicals and Plastics
- Textiles and Footwear
- Machinery
- Transportation
- Other

Note: Harmonized System (HS) sectors are an ad-hoc aggregation of the 21 HS sections.
Source: Database for Analysis of International Trade (BACI) (Gaulier and Zignago, 2010).

Figure 24: Welfare and Trade Impact of a Potential Free Trade Agreement with India

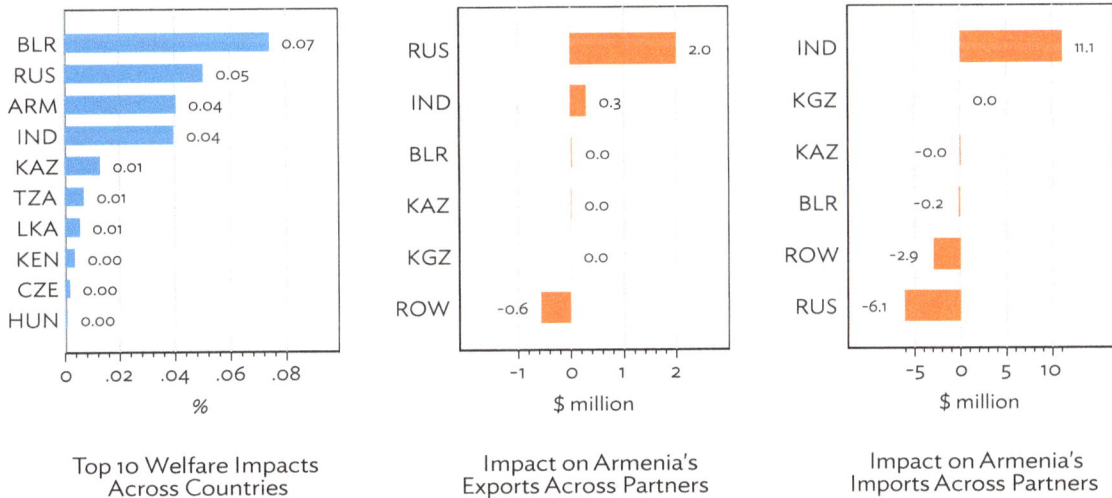

Top 10 Welfare Impacts Across Countries:
- BLR 0.07
- RUS 0.05
- ARM 0.04
- IND 0.04
- KAZ 0.01
- TZA 0.01
- LKA 0.01
- KEN 0.00
- CZE 0.00
- HUN 0.00

Impact on Armenia's Exports Across Partners ($ million):
- RUS 2.0
- IND 0.3
- BLR 0.0
- KAZ 0.0
- KGZ 0.0
- ROW -0.6

Impact on Armenia's Imports Across Partners ($ million):
- IND 11.1
- KGZ 0.0
- KAZ -0.0
- BLR -0.2
- ROW -2.9
- RUS -6.1

ROW = rest of the world.
Note: General equilibrium results. Three-letter codes are from the ISO 3166 standard.
Source: Asian Development Bank TA-9698 team calculation

Figure 25: Trade Impact of a Potential Free Trade Agreement with India, across Sectors

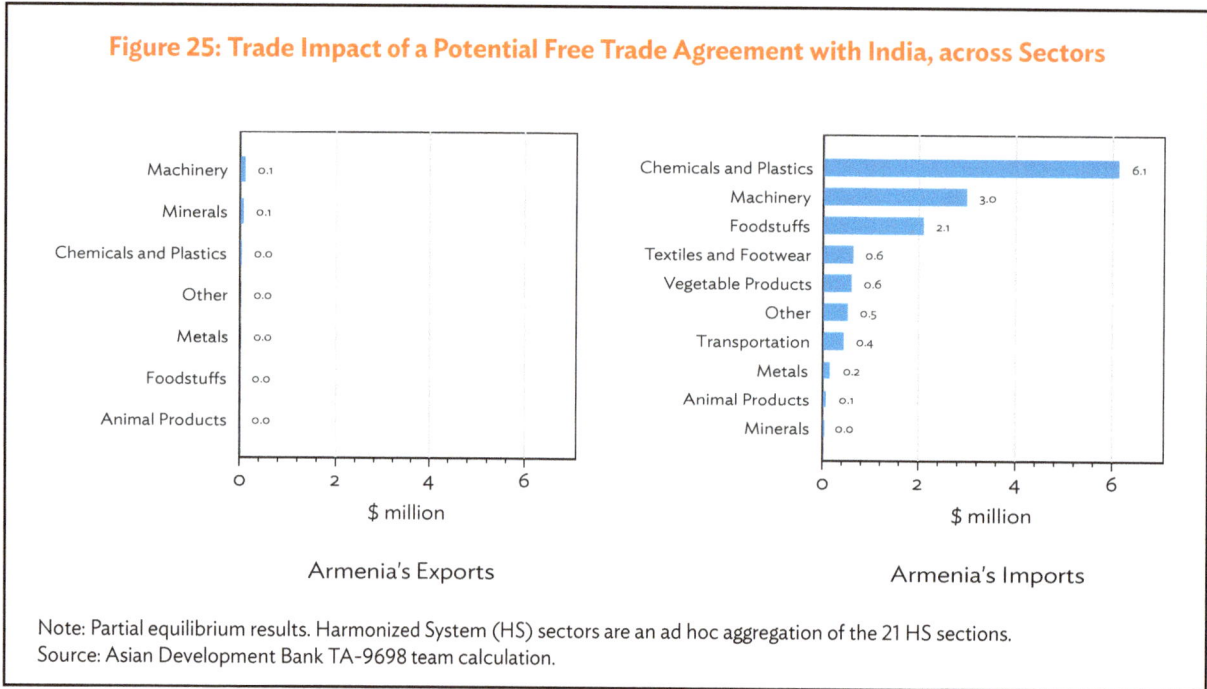

Armenia's Exports

Sector	$ million
Machinery	0.1
Minerals	0.1
Chemicals and Plastics	0.0
Other	0.0
Metals	0.0
Foodstuffs	0.0
Animal Products	0.0

Armenia's Imports

Sector	$ million
Chemicals and Plastics	6.1
Machinery	3.0
Foodstuffs	2.1
Textiles and Footwear	0.6
Vegetable Products	0.6
Other	0.5
Transportation	0.4
Metals	0.2
Animal Products	0.1
Minerals	0.0

Note: Partial equilibrium results. Harmonized System (HS) sectors are an ad hoc aggregation of the 21 HS sections.
Source: Asian Development Bank TA-9698 team calculation.

Figure 26: Trade Impact of a Potential Free Trade Agreement with India for the 10 Most-Affected Products

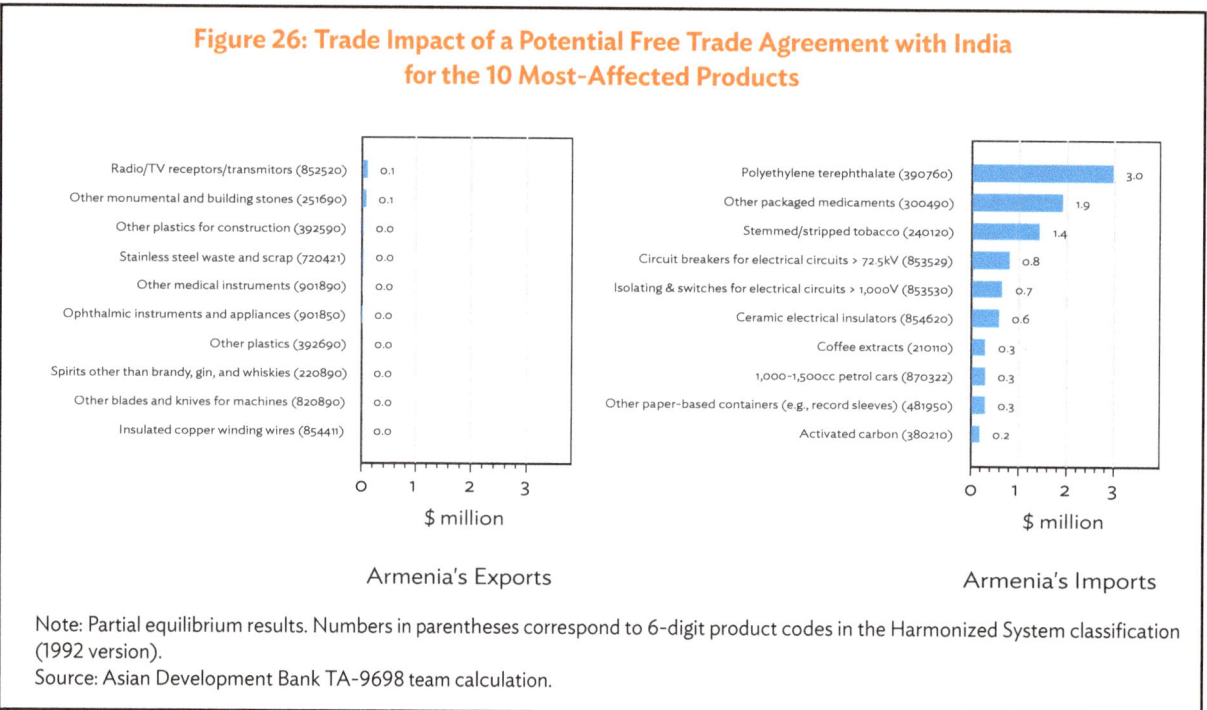

Armenia's Exports

Product	$ million
Radio/TV receptors/transmitors (852520)	0.1
Other monumental and building stones (251690)	0.1
Other plastics for construction (392590)	0.0
Stainless steel waste and scrap (720421)	0.0
Other medical instruments (901890)	0.0
Ophthalmic instruments and appliances (901850)	0.0
Other plastics (392690)	0.0
Spirits other than brandy, gin, and whiskies (220890)	0.0
Other blades and knives for machines (820890)	0.0
Insulated copper winding wires (854411)	0.0

Armenia's Imports

Product	$ million
Polyethylene terephthalate (390760)	3.0
Other packaged medicaments (300490)	1.9
Stemmed/stripped tobacco (240120)	1.4
Circuit breakers for electrical circuits > 72.5kV (853529)	0.8
Isolating & switches for electrical circuits > 1,000V (853530)	0.7
Ceramic electrical insulators (854620)	0.6
Coffee extracts (210110)	0.3
1,000–1,500cc petrol cars (870322)	0.3
Other paper-based containers (e.g., record sleeves) (481950)	0.3
Activated carbon (380210)	0.2

Note: Partial equilibrium results. Numbers in parentheses correspond to 6-digit product codes in the Harmonized System classification (1992 version).
Source: Asian Development Bank TA-9698 team calculation.

Impact of a Potential Free Trade Agreement with Iran

Negotiations for an EEU–Iran FTA could conclude in 2021. The EEU and Iran signed an interim agreement at the Astana Economic Forum on 17 May 2018, which came into force on 27 October 2019. The agreement includes tariff reductions for 4% of tariff lines, including complete removals for some products.[38] During a visit in Moscow in February 2021, the speaker of Iran's parliament indicated interest for Iran to become a permanent member of the EEU (IRNA, 2020; Latypova, 2020).

Armenia's imports from Iran largely exceed its exports to Iran, but exports have increased rapidly in recent years. Armenia's bilateral trade balance with Iran is in strong deficit (Figure 27). Mineral products account for 48% of bilateral imports ($121 million), including natural gas ($71 million), cement ($21 million), and crude oil ($13 million). Other key imports include chemicals and plastics ($45 million, of which $27 million is plastics) and base metals ($39 million, mostly iron and steel). In the other direction, lamb accounts for 79% of Armenia's exports to Iran ($14 million). This export-oriented value chain has driven the increase of bilateral exports since 2015.

General equilibrium: An EEU–Iran FTA would significantly increase Armenia's welfare and manufacturing trade. The general equilibrium analysis shows that an FTA with Iran would increase Armenia's welfare by 0.3%—roughly half the impact of an FTA with the PRC, but eight times more than an FTA with India. Armenia would reap the largest benefits among EEU members, far ahead of Kazakhstan, the Kyrgyz Republic, and the Russian Federation (+0.02% each) (Figure 28). Armenia's manufacturing exports to Iran would increase by $22 million (+26%), at the expense of a modest reduction of exports to the Russian Federation (–$2 million) and to the rest of the world (–$6 million). Armenia's manufacturing imports from Iran would increase by $42 million (+21%), also partly at the expense of imports from the Russian Federation (–$10 million) and the rest of the world (–$18 million).

Partial equilibrium: An EEU–Iran FTA would boost Armenia's exports of small trucks, chemicals and chocolate, and imports of plastics, asphalt, metals, and fertilizers. The partial equilibrium trade impact exceeds the impact in general equilibrium. Armenia's exports to Iran would be multiplied by 2.6—from $18 to $56 million—exceeding the general equilibrium impact (+$22 million). At the same time, Armenia's imports from Iran would increase by $90 million (+37%), twice the $42 million impact in general equilibrium (Figure 29 and Figure 30). The increase of Armenia's exports of small trucks would be particularly large (+$31 million), due to the high level of Iran's tariffs on this product (40%). Other products with large expected increases include "other chemicals" (+$25 million) and foodstuffs (+$3 million, mostly chocolate products and biscuits). Armenia's imports of chemicals and plastics would increase by $36 million, including polyethylene (+$16 million)—a plastic used as food container—polypropylene (+$7 million), and fertilizers (+$5 million). Imports of mineral fuels would increase by $27 million—including $19 million for petroleum bitumen (asphalt)—and imports of metals would increase by $16 million, including iron and steel (+$5 million) and ferro-silicon (+$3 million).

---

[38] Annex 1 of the agreement specifies tariff reductions by the EEU for 502 tariff lines and by Iran for 360 tariff lines. Tariff lines are defined at the HS 10-digit level, which includes more than 12,000 products.

Figure 27: Sectoral Composition of Armenia-Iran Trade, 2008–2018

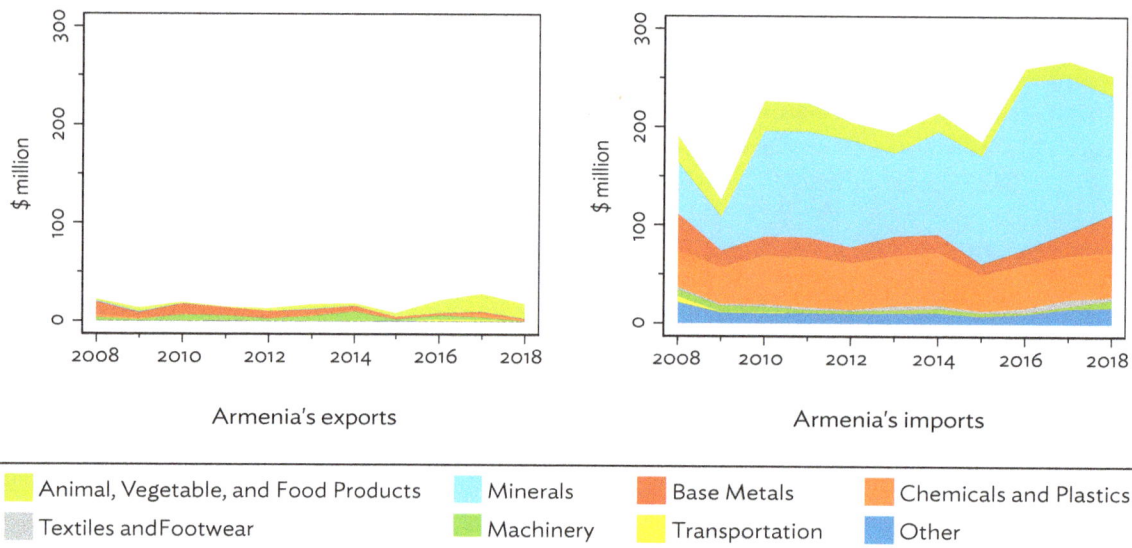

Armenia's exports

Armenia's imports

Animal, Vegetable, and Food Products | Minerals | Base Metals | Chemicals and Plastics
Textiles and Footwear | Machinery | Transportation | Other

Note: Harmonized System (HS) sectors are an ad hoc aggregation of the 21 HS sections.
Source: Database for Analysis of International Trade (BACI) (Gaulier and Zignago, 2010).

Figure 28: Welfare and Trade Impact of a Potential Free Trade Agreement with Iran

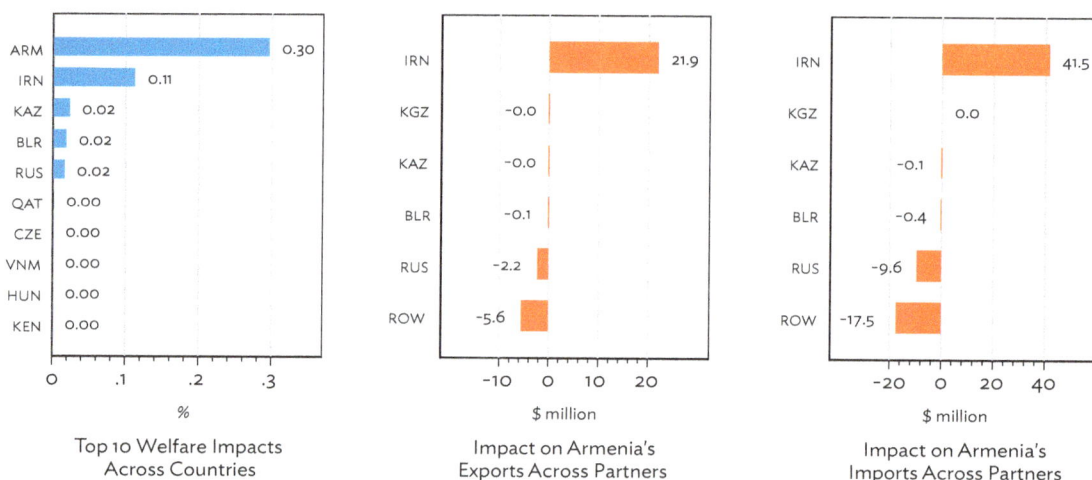

Top 10 Welfare Impacts
Across Countries

Impact on Armenia's
Exports Across Partners

Impact on Armenia's
Imports Across Partners

ROW = rest of the world.
Note: General equilibrium results. Three-letter codes are from the ISO 3166 standard.
Source: Asian Development Bank TA-9698 team calculation.

Figure 29: Trade Impact of a Potential Free Trade Agreement with Iran, across Sectors

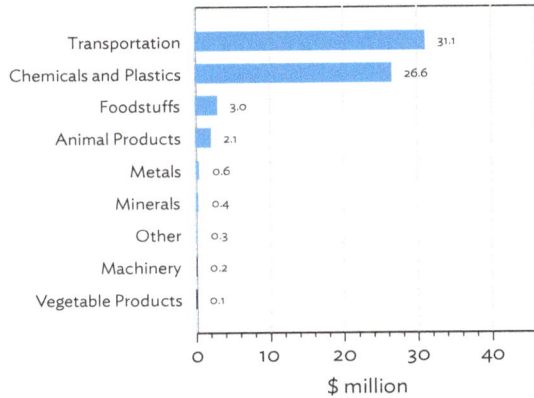

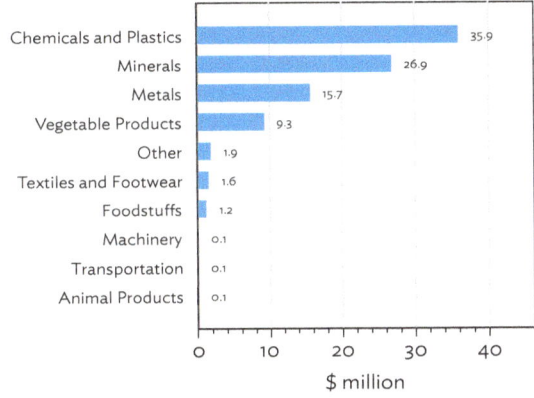

Armenia's Exports

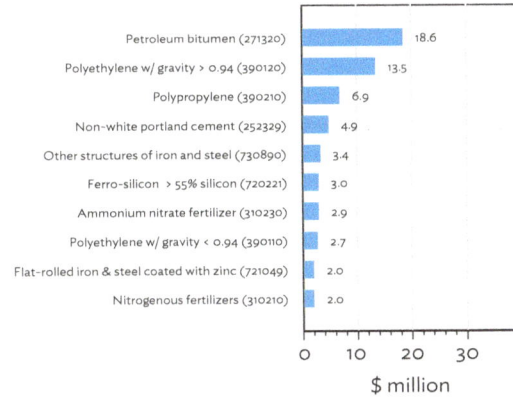

Sector	$ million
Transportation	31.1
Chemicals and Plastics	26.6
Foodstuffs	3.0
Animal Products	2.1
Metals	0.6
Minerals	0.4
Other	0.3
Machinery	0.2
Vegetable Products	0.1

Armenia's Imports

Sector	$ million
Chemicals and Plastics	35.9
Minerals	26.9
Metals	15.7
Vegetable Products	9.3
Other	1.9
Textiles and Footwear	1.6
Foodstuffs	1.2
Machinery	0.1
Transportation	0.1
Animal Products	0.1

Note: Partial equilibrium results. Harmonized System (HS) sectors are an ad-hoc aggregation of the 21 HS sections.
Source: Asian Development Bank TA-9698 team calculation.

Figure 30: Trade Impact of a Potential Free Trade Agreement with Iran for the 10 Most-Affected Products

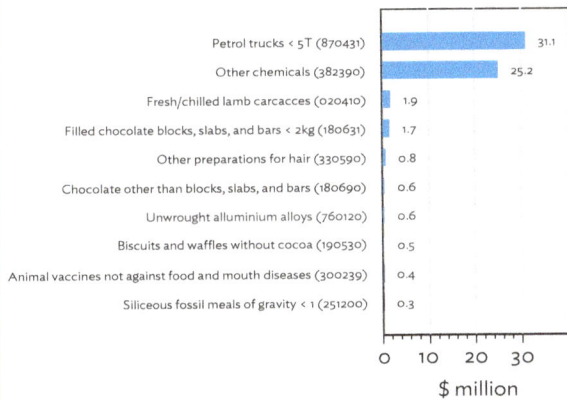

Armenia's Exports

Product	$ million
Petrol trucks < 5T (870431)	31.1
Other chemicals (382390)	25.2
Fresh/chilled lamb carcacces (020410)	1.9
Filled chocolate blocks, slabs, and bars < 2kg (180631)	1.7
Other preparations for hair (330590)	0.8
Chocolate other than blocks, slabs, and bars (180690)	0.6
Unwrought alluminium alloys (760120)	0.6
Biscuits and waffles without cocoa (190530)	0.5
Animal vaccines not against food and mouth diseases (300239)	0.4
Siliceous fossil meals of gravity < 1 (251200)	0.3

Armenia's Imports

Product	$ million
Petroleum bitumen (271320)	18.6
Polyethylene w/ gravity > 0.94 (390120)	13.5
Polypropylene (390210)	6.9
Non-white portland cement (252329)	4.9
Other structures of iron and steel (730890)	3.4
Ferro-silicon > 55% silicon (720221)	3.0
Ammonium nitrate fertilizer (310230)	2.9
Polyethylene w/ gravity < 0.94 (390110)	2.7
Flat-rolled iron & steel coated with zinc (721049)	2.0
Nitrogenous fertilizers (310210)	2.0

Note: Partial equilibrium results. Numbers in parentheses correspond to 6-digit product codes in the Harmonized System classification (1992 version).
Source: Asian Development Bank TA-9698 team calculation.

Impact of a Potential Free Trade Agreement with the People's Republic of China

Negotiations for an EEU–PRC FTA have not been initiated. The "Trade and Economic Cooperation Agreement" between the EEU and the PRC was signed at the Astana Economic Forum on 17 May 2018 and came into force on 25 October 2019. The agreement covers issues such as customs cooperation, technical barriers to trade and sanitary and phytosanitary, but it does not include any provision regarding preferential tariffs.

Machinery and textile imports from the PRC significantly exceed copper exports to the PRC. Armenia's bilateral trade balance with the PRC is in deficit (Figure 31). Machinery accounts for 45% of Armenia's imports from the PRC ($217 million), including televisions and video monitors ($57 million) as well as computers ($21 million). Other key imports include textiles and footwear ($76 million). Armenia mainly exports copper ores ($95 million) and non-knit clothing ($16 million) to the PRC.

General equilibrium: An EEU–PRC FTA would have a large impact on Armenia's welfare and manufacturing trade. The general equilibrium analysis indicates that an FTA with the PRC would increase Armenia's welfare by 0.7%, which is 18 times more than an FTA with India. Among EEU countries, the Kyrgyz Republic would reap the largest benefits, resulting in a 2.9% welfare increase, while Kazakhstan's welfare would increase by 1.1% (Figure 32).[39] Armenia's manufacturing exports to the PRC would increase by $12 million (+9%), partly at the expense of exports to the Russian Federation (–$8 million). Armenia's manufacturing imports from the PRC would increase by $98 million (+20%), partly at the expense of imports from the Russian Federation (–$22 million) and the rest of the world (–$64 million).

Partial equilibrium: An EEU–PRC FTA would boost Armenia's exports of cars and imports of household appliances, cars, trucks, bicycles, and car tires. The partial equilibrium trade impact exceeds the impact in general equilibrium. Armenia's exports to the PRC would increase by $48 million (+38%), against $12 million in general equilibrium. At the same time, Armenia's imports from the PRC would increase by $155 million (+32%), against $98 million in general equilibrium (Figure 33 and Figure 34). Armenia's exports would mostly increase for medium-sized cars (+$46 million)—although this might be an artefact as the counterfactual exercise relies on 2018 as the baseline, when Armenia's re-exports of used cars were abnormally large. Exports of textiles would also benefit from an FTA (+$2 million), particularly "non-knitted or crocheted men's track suits" (+$1 million). The increase in imports would be more diversified, starting with machinery (+$52 million)—including television sets (+$24 million), refrigerators (+$4 million), bicycles, and washing machines (+$3 million each). Imports would also increase for chemicals and plastics (+$25 million) and transportation (+$19 million), including mid-sized cars (+$6 million) and car tires (+$5 million).

---

[39]   This is linked to the intensity of existing trade as the PRC accounts for 53% of imports by the Kyrgyz Republic and 23% of imports by Kazakhstan.

Figure 31: Sectoral Composition of Armenia–People's Republic of China Trade, 2008–2018

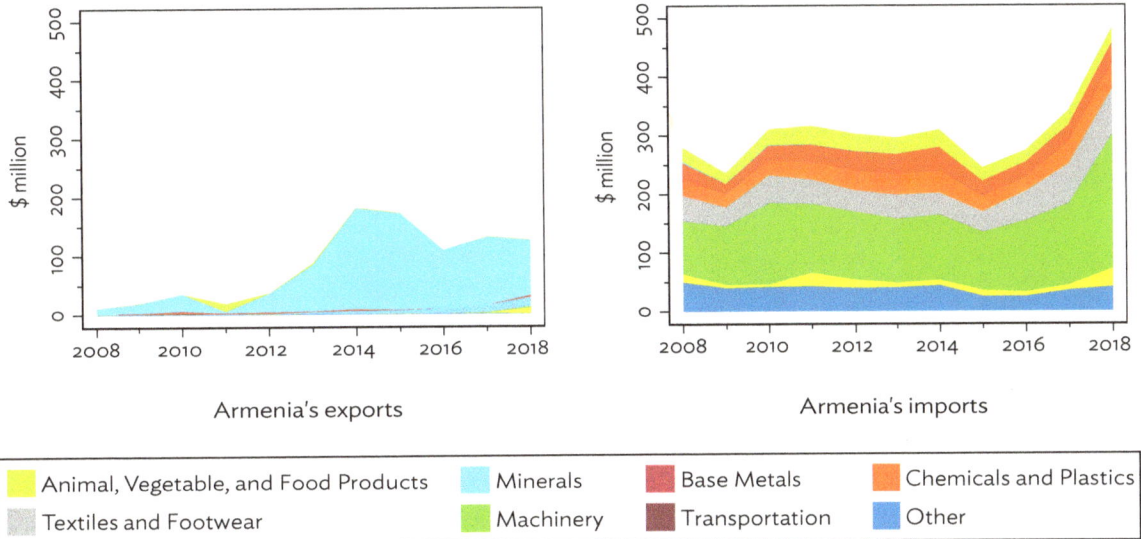

Armenia's exports

Armenia's imports

Legend:
- Animal, Vegetable, and Food Products
- Minerals
- Base Metals
- Chemicals and Plastics
- Textiles and Footwear
- Machinery
- Transportation
- Other

Note: Harmonized System (HS) sectors are an ad-hoc aggregation of the 21 HS sections.
Source: Database for Analysis of International Trade (BACI) (Gaulier and Zignago, 2010).

Figure 32: Welfare and Trade Impact of a Potential Free Trade Agreement with the People's Republic of China

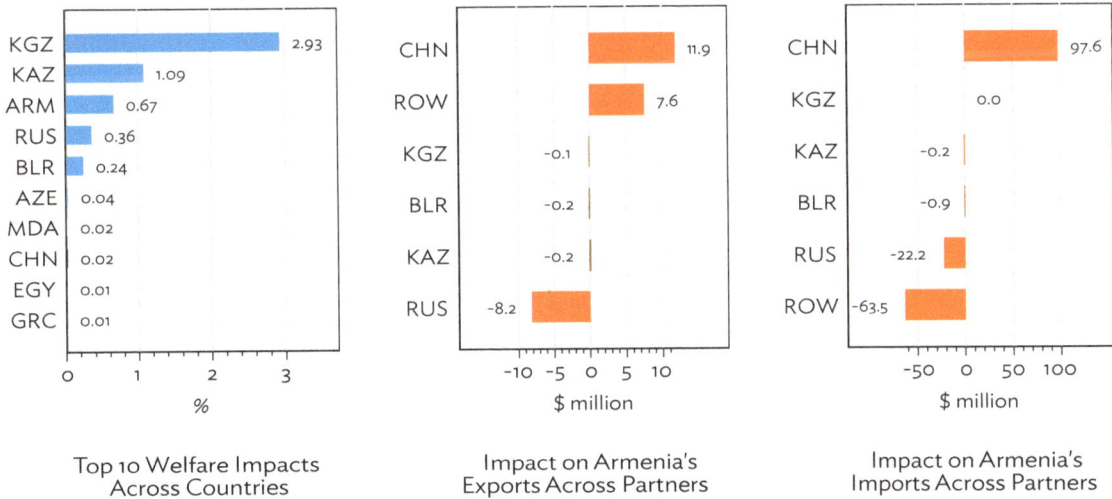

Top 10 Welfare Impacts Across Countries

	%
KGZ	2.93
KAZ	1.09
ARM	0.67
RUS	0.36
BLR	0.24
AZE	0.04
MDA	0.02
CHN	0.02
EGY	0.01
GRC	0.01

Impact on Armenia's Exports Across Partners

	$ million
CHN	11.9
ROW	7.6
KGZ	-0.1
BLR	-0.2
KAZ	-0.2
RUS	-8.2

Impact on Armenia's Imports Across Partners

	$ million
CHN	97.6
KGZ	0.0
KAZ	-0.2
BLR	-0.9
RUS	-22.2
ROW	-63.5

ROW = rest of the world.
Note: General equilibrium results. Three-letter codes are from the ISO 3166 standard.
Source: Asian Development Bank TA-9698 team calculation

Figure 33: Trade Impact of a Potential Free Trade Agreement with the People's Republic of China, across Sectors

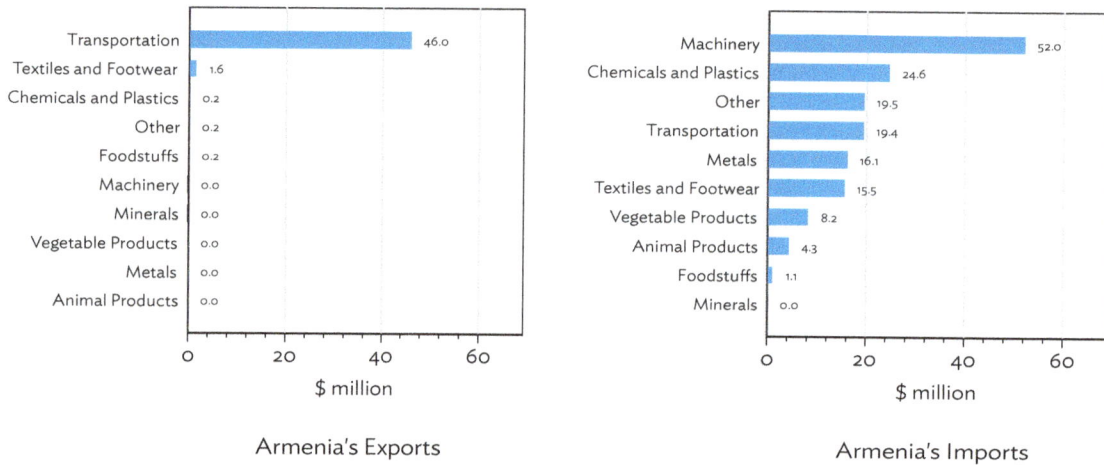

Armenia's Exports

Sector	$ million
Transportation	46.0
Textiles and Footwear	1.6
Chemicals and Plastics	0.2
Other	0.2
Foodstuffs	0.2
Machinery	0.0
Minerals	0.0
Vegetable Products	0.0
Metals	0.0
Animal Products	0.0

Armenia's Imports

Sector	$ million
Machinery	52.0
Chemicals and Plastics	24.6
Other	19.5
Transportation	19.4
Metals	16.1
Textiles and Footwear	15.5
Vegetable Products	8.2
Animal Products	4.3
Foodstuffs	1.1
Minerals	0.0

Note: Partial equilibrium results. Harmonized System (HS) sectors are an ad-hoc aggregation of the 21 sections.
Source: Asian Development Bank TA-9698 team calculation.

Figure 34: Trade Impact of a Potential Free Trade Agreement with the People's Republic of China for the 10 Most-Affected Products

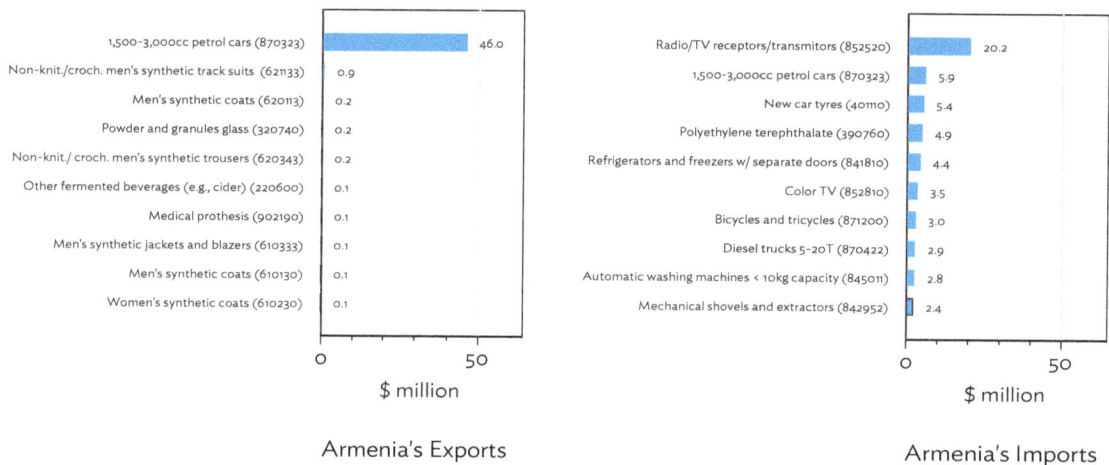

Armenia's Exports

Product	$ million
1,500–3,000cc petrol cars (870323)	46.0
Non-knit./croch. men's synthetic track suits (621133)	0.9
Men's synthetic coats (620113)	0.2
Powder and granules glass (320740)	0.2
Non-knit./croch. men's synthetic trousers (620343)	0.2
Other fermented beverages (e.g., cider) (220600)	0.1
Medical prothesis (902190)	0.1
Men's synthetic jackets and blazers (610333)	0.1
Men's synthetic coats (610130)	0.1
Women's synthetic coats (610230)	0.1

Armenia's Imports

Product	$ million
Radio/TV receptors/transmitors (852520)	20.2
1,500–3,000cc petrol cars (870323)	5.9
New car tyres (401110)	5.4
Polyethylene terephthalate (390760)	4.9
Refrigerators and freezers w/ separate doors (841810)	4.4
Color TV (852810)	3.5
Bicycles and tricycles (871200)	3.0
Diesel trucks 5-20T (870422)	2.9
Automatic washing machines < 10kg capacity (845011)	2.8
Mechanical shovels and extractors (842952)	2.4

Note: Partial equilibrium results. Numbers in parentheses correspond to 6-digit product codes in the Harmonized System classification (1992 version).
Source: Asian Development Bank TA-9698 team calculation.

Impact of the Free Trade Agreement with Serbia

Signed in October 2019, the FTA is expected to have a minor impact on Armenia. The EEU–Serbia FTA was signed on 25 October 2019 and ratified by all EEU members, including Armenia on 19 April 2021, and it should enter into force by mid-2021. The FTA covers the vast majority of products, but it excludes some of them, including two key export products for Armenia—brandy and cigarettes.[40] It is also important to note that the EEU–Serbia FTA will have to be terminated if Serbia joins the EU, which is currently expected before 2030.

Serbia is the destination of 4.3% of Armenia's exports, while it is the origin of only 0.1% of imports. Armenia's bilateral trade balance with Iran is in strong surplus, due to a large and recent increase in copper exports, accounting for close to 100% of Armenia's bilateral exports in 2018 ($121 million) (Figure 35). On the other hand, Armenia imports less than $3 million per year from Serbia, with tobacco accounting for 21% of imports and pharmaceutical products accounting for 17%.

General equilibrium: Armenia's welfare and manufacturing trade will be virtually unaffected by the FTA. The general equilibrium analysis shows that an FTA with Serbia would increase Armenia's welfare by less than 0.005%, with Serbia's welfare only increasing by 0.09% (Figure 36). Armenia's imports would be virtually unaffected as the existing trade flows are minimal; and the impact on Armenia's exports would also be minimal as Serbia's tariff on copper is already very low (1%).

Partial equilibrium results corroborate the limited expected impact of the FTA. Partial equilibrium results across products corroborate general equilibrium results, including a minimal impact on Armenia's exports to Serbia—entirely concentrated on aluminium foil—and very limited impact on Armenia's imports, with the impact concentrating on chemicals and plastics (mostly pharmaceutical products) and vegetable products (mostly cigarettes, which are in any case subject to a tariff-rate quota).[41]

---

[40] Annexes 1 and 2 of the FTA list the exceptions that apply to Serbia's imports from the EEU and the EEU's imports from Serbia. Of particular relevance to Armenia, the FTA maintains a tariff-rate quota (i.e., duty free only for a certain quantity) for brandy and cigarettes originating from all EEU members, except the Russian Federation, which is exempted.

[41] For more information on this, refer to footnote 40.

Figure 35: Sectoral Composition of Armenia–Serbia Trade, 2008–2018

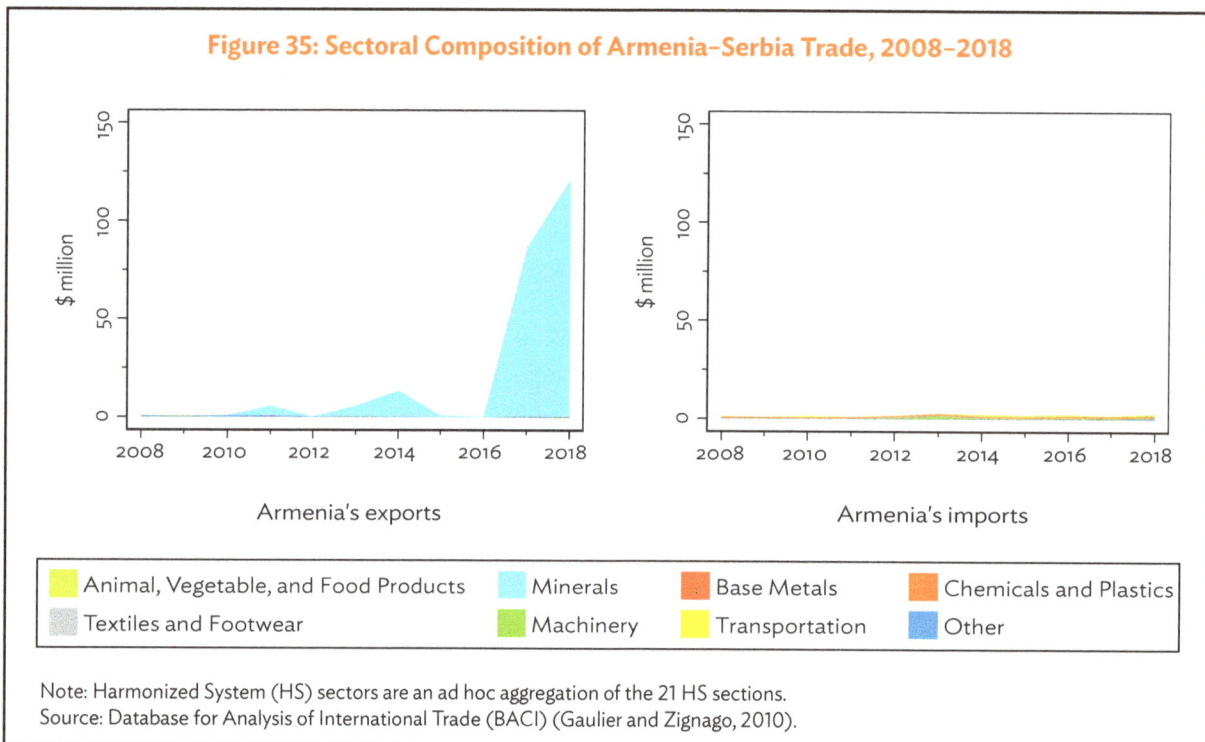

Armenia's exports

Armenia's imports

- Animal, Vegetable, and Food Products
- Minerals
- Base Metals
- Chemicals and Plastics
- Textiles and Footwear
- Machinery
- Transportation
- Other

Note: Harmonized System (HS) sectors are an ad hoc aggregation of the 21 HS sections.
Source: Database for Analysis of International Trade (BACI) (Gaulier and Zignago, 2010).

Figure 36: Welfare and Trade Impact of the Free Trade Agreement with Serbia

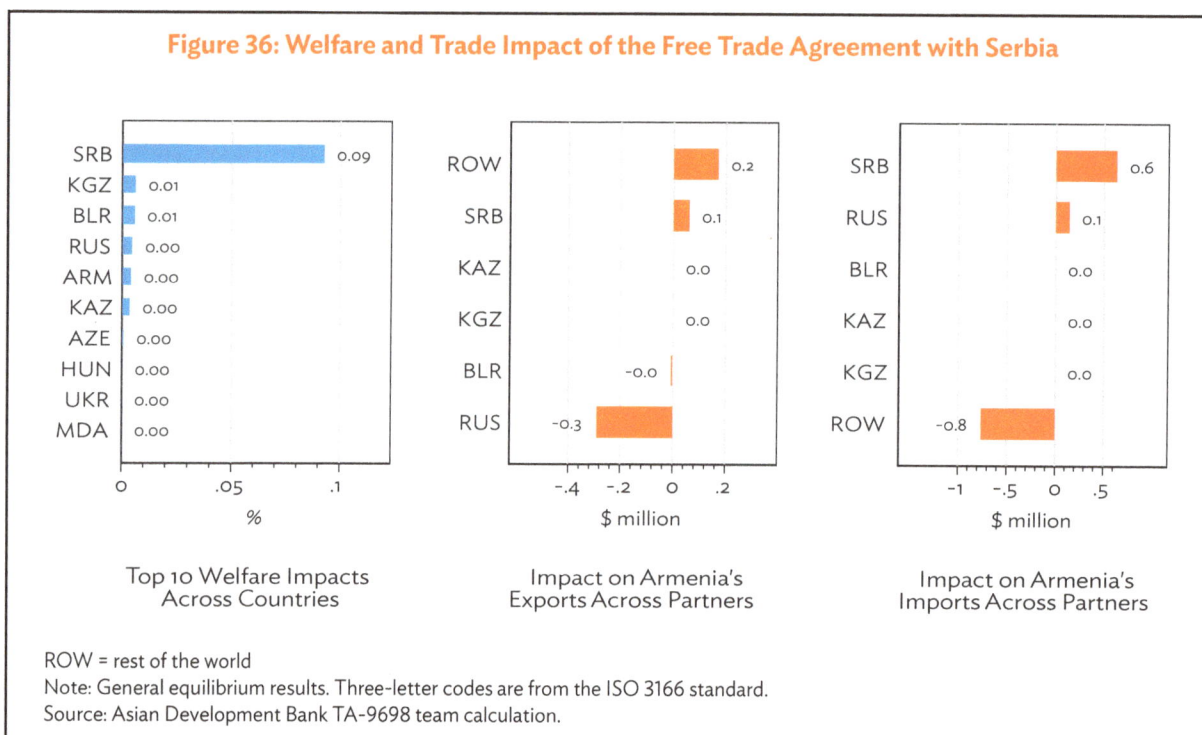

Top 10 Welfare Impacts Across Countries

	%
SRB	0.09
KGZ	0.01
BLR	0.01
RUS	0.00
ARM	0.00
KAZ	0.00
AZE	0.00
HUN	0.00
UKR	0.00
MDA	0.00

Impact on Armenia's Exports Across Partners

	$ million
ROW	0.2
SRB	0.1
KAZ	0.0
KGZ	0.0
BLR	-0.0
RUS	-0.3

Impact on Armenia's Imports Across Partners

	$ million
SRB	0.6
RUS	0.1
BLR	0.0
KAZ	0.0
KGZ	0.0
ROW	-0.8

ROW = rest of the world
Note: General equilibrium results. Three-letter codes are from the ISO 3166 standard.
Source: Asian Development Bank TA-9698 team calculation.

Figure 37: Trade Impact of the Free Trade Agreement with Serbia, across Sectors

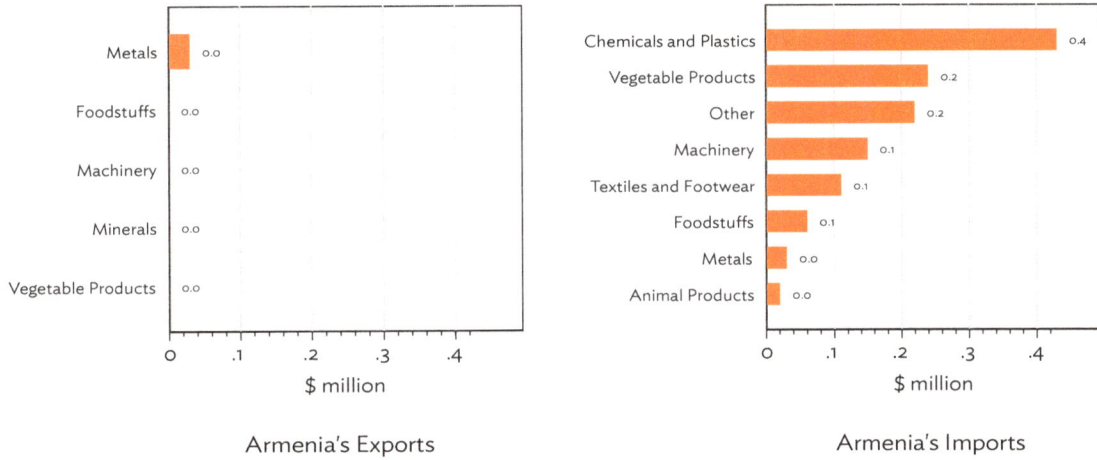

Armenia's Exports

Sector	$ million
Metals	0.0
Foodstuffs	0.0
Machinery	0.0
Minerals	0.0
Vegetable Products	0.0

Armenia's Imports

Sector	$ million
Chemicals and Plastics	0.4
Vegetable Products	0.2
Other	0.2
Machinery	0.1
Textiles and Footwear	0.1
Foodstuffs	0.1
Metals	0.0
Animal Products	0.0

Note: Partial equilibrium results. Harmonized System (HS) sectors are an ad hoc aggregation of the 21 HS sections.
Source: Asian Development Bank TA-9698 team calculation.

Figure 38: Trade Impact of the Free Trade Agreement with Serbia for the 10 Most-Affected Products

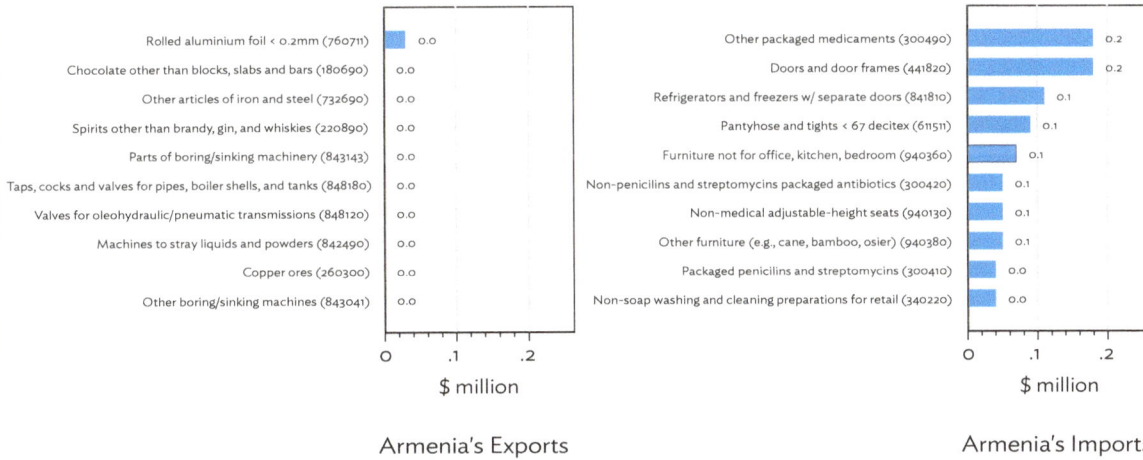

Armenia's Exports

Product	$ million
Rolled aluminium foil < 0.2mm (760711)	0.0
Chocolate other than blocks, slabs and bars (180690)	0.0
Other articles of iron and steel (732690)	0.0
Spirits other than brandy, gin, and whiskies (220890)	0.0
Parts of boring/sinking machinery (843143)	0.0
Taps, cocks and valves for pipes, boiler shells, and tanks (848180)	0.0
Valves for oleohydraulic/pneumatic transmissions (848120)	0.0
Machines to stray liquids and powders (842490)	0.0
Copper ores (260300)	0.0
Other boring/sinking machines (843041)	0.0

Armenia's Imports

Product	$ million
Other packaged medicaments (300490)	0.2
Doors and door frames (441820)	0.2
Refrigerators and freezers w/ separate doors (841810)	0.1
Pantyhose and tights < 67 decitex (611511)	0.1
Furniture not for office, kitchen, bedroom (940360)	0.1
Non-penicilins and streptomycins packaged antibiotics (300420)	0.1
Non-medical adjustable-height seats (940130)	0.1
Other furniture (e.g., cane, bamboo, osier) (940380)	0.1
Packaged penicilins and streptomycins (300410)	0.0
Non-soap washing and cleaning preparations for retail (340220)	0.0

Note: Partial equilibrium results. Numbers in parentheses correspond to 6-digit product codes in the Harmonized System classification (1992 version).
Source: Asian Development Bank TA-9698 team calculation.

Impact of the Loss of European Union Generalised Scheme of Preferences Eligibility

Armenia should lose its eligibility for the EU's GSP and GSP+ in January 2022. As explained in the background section, Armenia should stop benefiting from the EU's GSP in January 2022. The loss of GSP eligibility will include GSP (duty reductions for 66% of tariff lines, applicable to 71 developing countries) as well as GSP+ (zero duties for 66% of tariff lines, applicable to nine countries that have implemented a set of 27 international conventions on human and labor rights, environmental protection and good governance) (EU Commission, 2020a). This section estimates the welfare and export impact of the loss of GSP and GSP+ status for Armenia.

Armenia imports a wide range of products from the EU, but it mostly exports copper. Armenia's bilateral trade balance with the EU remains in deficit, despite increased copper exports since 2015 (Figure 39). Imports from the EU fell in 2015–2016 as GDP growth slowed down in Armenia, but they quickly recovered, particularly as industrial machinery imports picked up to support the development of the agribusiness sector, including spirits, cigarettes and confectionery manufacturing, as well as greenhouse farming.

General equilibrium: Armenia's welfare should decrease by 0.1% and exports to the EU should fall by $35 million. The export contraction corresponds to 9% of Armenia's manufacturing exports to the EU. This limited contraction is largely due to EU MFN tariffs being low for most of the manufactured products that Armenia exports, and notably copper products (0%) and ferro-molybdenum alloys (2.7%). The effective tariff increases due to the loss of GSP eligibility are thus limited. However, these results should be considered as lower bounds approximations of the real effect as they were obtained based on exports to a subset of 17 EU countries, accounting for 62% of Armenia's manufacturing exports to the EU.[42] Armenia's manufacturing exports to Germany are expected to be the most affected (–$23 million), followed by Italy (–$6 million) and France (–$2 million). Foregone exports to the EU are also expected to be partially reallocated to the Russian Federation (+$9 million).

Partial equilibrium: Armenia's exports could fall by $156 million. As the general equilibrium analysis is restricted to manufacturing trade, which only accounts for 58% of Armenia's exports to the EU in 2018, it is helpful to turn to the partial equilibrium analysis to assess the overall impact. The loss of GSP benefits is then estimated to reduce Armenia's exports to the EU by $156 million (–19%).[43] Exports to Germany are expected to decline the most (–$59 million), followed by the Netherlands (–$57 million) (Figure 41). Exports of metals are expected to decline the most (–$139 million), particularly ferro-molybdenum alloy exports and exports of aluminium foil (Figure 42 and Figure 43). Exports of textiles are also expected to decline by $16 million, largely men's cotton and synthetic fiber trousers and coats. These products all make up a large share of Armenia's exports to the EU and their exports are either very elastic to tariff increases (e.g., ferro-molybdenum alloy has a tariff elasticity of –21) or will face high tariffs once Armenia's exports are subject to the EU's MFN (e.g., the EU's MFN for non-knitted clothing is 12%).

---

[42]   The 17 countries include Austria, Bulgaria, Croatia, the Czech Republic, Denmark, Finland, France, Germany, Greece, Hungary, Italy, Poland, Portugal, Romania, Spain, Sweden, and the United Kingdom (included as part of the EU).

[43]   The trade impact in partial equilibrium is larger than in general equilibrium. The gap is not only due to the goods coverage as it still holds when the analysis is restricted to manufacturing trade. This is because the general equilibrium analysis relies on a single tariff elasticity average while the partial equilibrium analysis relies on tariff elasticities at the 6-digit product level. This creates an aggregation bias that minimizes general equilibrium impacts, as explained in Ossa (2015).

Figure 39: Sectoral Composition of Armenia–European Union Trade, 2008–2018

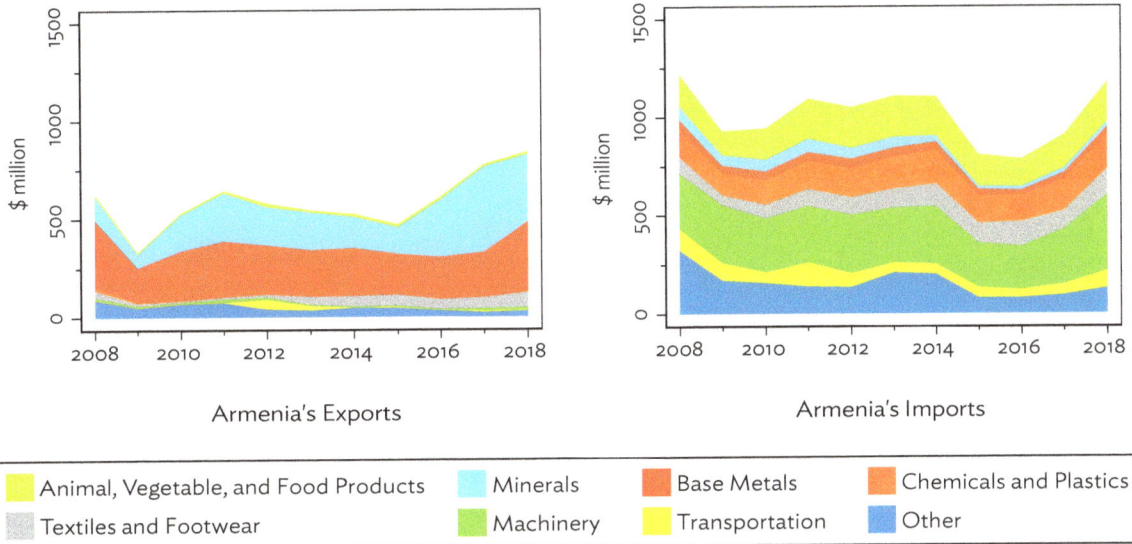

Armenia's Exports

Armenia's Imports

- Animal, Vegetable, and Food Products
- Minerals
- Base Metals
- Chemicals and Plastics
- Textiles and Footwear
- Machinery
- Transportation
- Other

Note: Harmonized System (HS) sectors are an ad hoc aggregation of the 21 HS sections.
Source: Database for Analysis of International Trade (BACI) (Gaulier and Zignago, 2010)

Figure 40: Welfare and Trade Impact of the Loss of EU GSP Eligibility

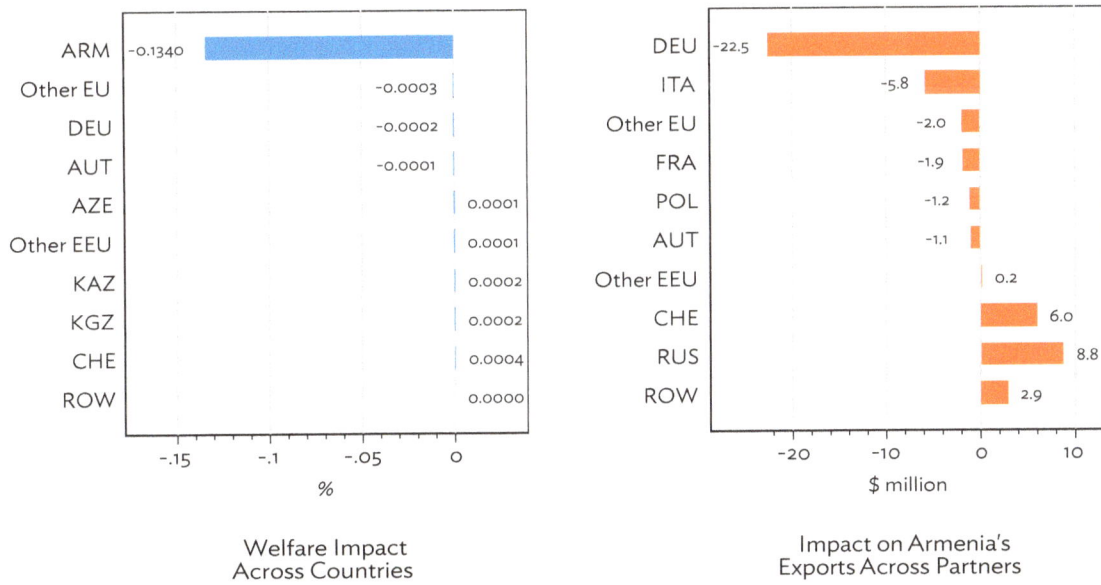

Welfare Impact Across Countries	
ARM	−0.1340
Other EU	−0.0003
DEU	−0.0002
AUT	−0.0001
AZE	0.0001
Other EEU	0.0001
KAZ	0.0002
KGZ	0.0002
CHE	0.0004
ROW	0.0000

Impact on Armenia's Exports Across Partners	
DEU	−22.5
ITA	−5.8
Other EU	−2.0
FRA	−1.9
POL	−1.2
AUT	−1.1
Other EEU	0.2
CHE	6.0
RUS	8.8
ROW	2.9

Welfare Impact
Across Countries

Impact on Armenia's
Exports Across Partners

EU = European Union, EEU = Eurasian Economic Union, GSP = Generalised Scheme of Preferences, ROW = rest of the world.
Note: General equilibrium results. Three-letter codes are from the ISO 3166 standard.
Source: Asian Development Bank TA-9698 team calculation.

Figure 41: Impact of the Loss of EU GSP Eligibility on Armenia's Exports, across Destinations

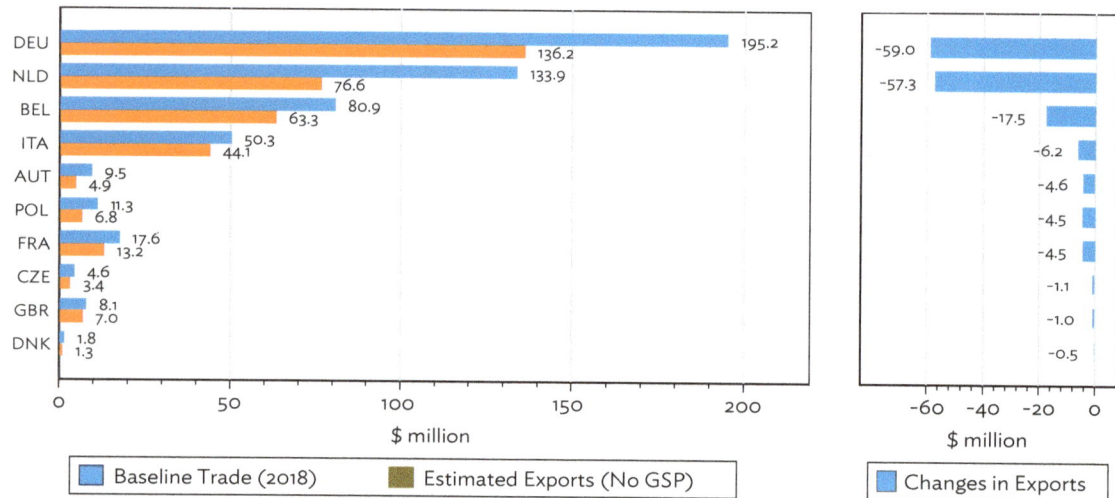

	Baseline Trade (2018)	Estimated Exports (No GSP)	Changes in Exports
DEU	195.2	136.2	-59.0
NLD	133.9	76.6	-57.3
BEL	80.9	63.3	-17.5
ITA	50.3	44.1	-6.2
AUT	9.5	4.9	-4.6
POL	11.3	6.8	-4.5
FRA	17.6	13.2	-4.5
CZE	4.6	3.4	-1.1
GBR	8.1	7.0	-1.0
DNK	1.8	1.3	-0.5

$ million

EU = European Union, GSP = Generalised Scheme of Preferences.
Note: Partial equilibrium results. Three-letter codes are from the ISO 3166 standard.
Source: Asian Development Bank TA-9698 team calculation.

Figure 42: Impact of the Loss of EU GSP Eligibility on Armenia's Export, across Sectors

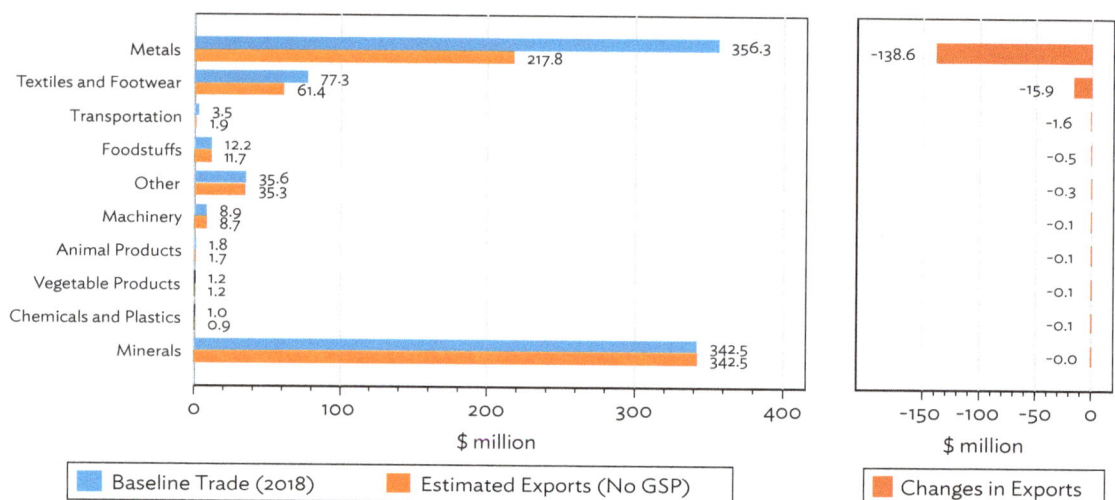

	Baseline Trade (2018)	Estimated Exports (No GSP)	Changes in Exports
Metals	356.3	217.8	-138.6
Textiles and Footwear	77.3	61.4	-15.9
Transportation	3.5	1.9	-1.6
Foodstuffs	12.2	11.7	-0.5
Other	35.6	35.3	-0.3
Machinery	8.9	8.7	-0.1
Animal Products	1.8	1.7	-0.1
Vegetable Products	1.2	1.2	-0.1
Chemicals and Plastics	1.0	0.9	-0.1
Minerals	342.5	342.5	-0.0

$ million

EU = European Union, GSP = Generalised Scheme of Preferences.
Note: Partial equilibrium results. Harmonized System (HS) sectors are an ad hoc aggregation of the 21 HS sections.
Source: Asian Development Bank TA-9698 team calculation.

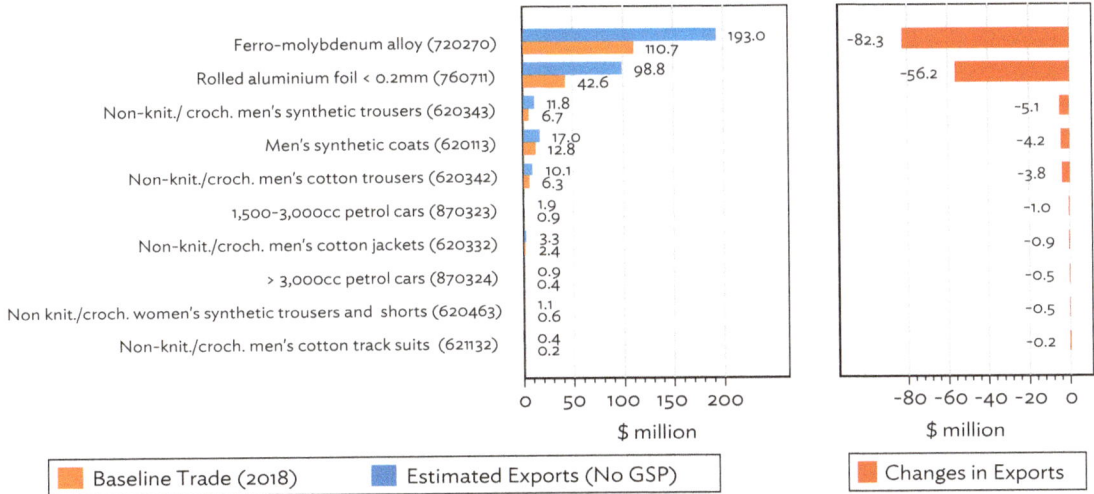

Figure 43: Impact of the Loss of EU GSP Eligibility on Armenia's Exports for the 10 Most-Affected Products

GSP = Generalised Scheme of Preferences.
Note: Partial equilibrium results. Numbers in parentheses correspond to 6-digit product codes in the Harmonized System classification (1992 version).
Source: Asian Development Bank TA-9698 team calculation.

VI. Conclusions

The convergence to the EEU CET is expected to reduce Armenia's welfare by 1.6%. This reduction arises from tariff increases due to the alignment to the CET. These tariff increases are in turn expected to reduce imports of manufactured goods by $145 million. Convergence to the CET is also expected to generate $90 million additional imports from EEU and FTA partners. In net terms, EEU membership is thus expected to reduce imports by $54 million every year, by the end of the transition period.

Sectors will be affected differently. Imports of chemicals and plastics are expected to decline the most with the overall convergence to the CET, including medicaments and plastics used in agribusiness. On the other hand, imports of food products (excluding meat) and machinery should be relatively spared.

The tariff changes implemented on 1 January 2021 and 1 January 2022 are expected to have a minimal impact. The tariff changes of 1 January 2021 are expected to generate a limited decrease in imports, concentrated in medicaments and plastics. The tariff changes of 1 January 2022 are expected to generate an even smaller decline in imports, almost entirely concentrating on frozen pork.

EEU membership provides new opportunities for FTAs that could increase Armenia's welfare by 1.0%. Significant gains would be made if FTAs provide duty-free access to all goods, including chemicals and confectionery. FTAs with the PRC and Iran would 'generate the largest gains for Armenia. An FTA with these countries might be particularly attractive for both sides as imports from the PRC and Iran are also among those that will suffer the most from Armenia's convergence to the EEU CET.

The loss of EU GSP eligibility is expected to reduce Armenia's welfare by 0.1%. The loss of GSP benefits is also estimated to reduce manufacturing exports to the EU by $35 million (general equilibrium) to $156 million (partial equilibrium). Exports of ferro-molybdenum alloys and aluminium foil to Belgium, Germany, and the Netherlands are expected to decline the most.

Possible policy actions. Policymakers need to assess which producers and consumers are likely to be affected by the import reductions. For instance, if imports of these products are used as inputs in the production of other goods, a selective duty drawback scheme could be introduced to offset the tariff hikes.[44] Instead, if imports are used for domestic consumption or investment, alternative responses could be more suitable, such as selective value-added tax reductions. This report also highlights the critical importance of a limited range of products for Armenia to reap benefits from the FTAs negotiated by the EEU. It is therefore critical that these products are systematically covered by the FTAs.

---

[44] Duty drawbacks compensate tariffs on inputs used in the production of export goods. Such a scheme can increase the competitiveness of domestic producers in the presence of large import tariffs.

Appendix: Descriptive Statistics

Table A1: Main Products Exported by Armenia to Top Destinations, 2018

Destination[a]		Exports		Top Products[b]	
		$ million	% of Total	Product	% of Bilateral
European Union,		840	29.5	Copper	44
of which	Bulgaria	215	7.5	Molybdenum	24
	Germany	195	6.9	Aluminium foil	12
	Netherlands	134	4.7	Textiles	9
	Belgium	81	2.8	Zinc	3
Russian Federation		661	23.2	Brandy	24
				Textiles	22
				Diamonds	5
				Trout	3
				Tomatoes	3
Switzerland		506	17.8	Gold	66
				Copper	26
				Watch cases	4
Iraq		151	5.3	Cigarettes	97
People's Republic of China		126	4.4	Copper	77
				Textiles	13
Serbia		121	4.3	Copper	100
United Arab Emirates		76	2.7	Cigarettes	45
				Precious-metal jewelry	27
Georgia		76	2.7	Cigarettes	18
				Glass pots and bottles	14
United States		57	2.0	Aluminium foil	42
Syria		56	2.0	Cigarettes	100
Canada		37	1.3	Copper	60
Total		2,707	95%		

HS = Harmonized System classification (1992 version).
[a] This table reports exports to the 11 destinations that absorb at least 1% of Armenia's exports.
[b] Top products report the breakdown across products accounting for at least 3% of bilateral exports and at least $10 million value. Products are defined as follows: copper (HS 2-digits = 72 or HS 4-digits = 2603), molybdenum (HS 4-digits = 2613 or HS 6-digits = 720270), aluminium foil (HS 4-digits = 7607), textiles (HS 2-digits = 50–63), zinc (HS 4-digits = 2608), brandy (HS 6-digits = 220820), diamonds (HS 4-digits = 7202), trout (HS 6-digits = 030211), tomatoes (HS 6-digits = 070200), gold (HS 4-digits = 7108), watch cases (HS 4-digits = 9111), cigarettes (HS 6-digits = 240220), precious-metal jewelry (HS 4-digits = 7113), glass pots and bottles (HS 4-digits = 7010).
Source: Database for Analysis of International Trade (BACI) (Gaulier and Zignago, 2010).

Table A2:   Main Destinations for Armenia's Top Export Products, 2018

Product	Exports		Top Destinations[a]	
	$ million	% of Total	Product[b]	% of Bilateral
Copper	763	26.8	European Union	49
			Switzerland	17
			Serbia	16
			People's Republic of China	13
			Canada	3
Gold	344	12.1	Switzerland	97
Textiles	286	10.1	Russian Federation	51
			European Union	27
			People's Republic of China	6
			Japan	5
Cigarettes	265	9.3	Iraq	55
			Syria	21
			United Arab Emirates	13
			Georgia	5
Molybdenum	215	7.5	European Union	93
			Chile	5
Brandy	190	6.7	Russian Federation	85
Aluminium Foil	127	4.5	European Union	81
			United States	19
Diamonds	83	2.9	Russian Federation	38
			European Union	25
Precious-metal jewelry	40	1.4	United Arab Emirates	51
Total	2,313	82.0%		

HS = Harmonized System classification (1992 version).

[a] 'Top destinations' report the breakdown across destination economies accounting for at least 1% of exports.

[b] Products are defined as per the HS classification: copper (HS 2-digits = 72 or HS 4-digits = 2603), molybdenum (HS 4-digits = 2613 or HS 6-digits = 720270), aluminium foil (HS 4-digits = 7607), textiles (HS 2-digits = 50–63), brandy (HS 6-digits = 220820), diamonds (HS 4-digits = 7202), gold (HS 4-digits = 7108), cigarettes (HS 6-digits = 240220), precious-metal jewelry (HS 4-digits = 7113).

Source: Database for Analysis of International Trade (BACI) (Gaulier and Zignago, 2010).

Table A3:   Tariffs on Armenia's Exports of Top HS 6-Digit Products, as per Eurasian Economic Union Bilateral Trade Agreements

HS 6-digit code	Product	Share in Armenia's exports (2017)	FTA with Viet Nam		Interim FTA with Iran		FTA with Serbia	
			MFN	FTA	MFN	FTA	MFN	FTA
260300	Copper ores	34.7%	0%	0%	5%	5%	1%	0%
240220	Cigarettes	9.5%	135%	135%	26%	26%	15%	0% up to 2 billion units per year[a]
220820	Spirits obtained by distilling wine, grape marc	8.1%	45%	45%	—	—	30%	0% up to 50,000 liters of pure alcohol per year[b]
710812	Non-monetary gold in unwrought forms	5.8%	0%	0%	5%	5%	3%	0%
760711	Aluminium foil < 0.2mm	4.8%	0%	0%	5%	5%	5%	0%
720270	Ferro-molybdenum alloys	3.7%	0%	0%	15%	15%	0%	0%
740200	Unrefined copper	2.9%	0%	0%	5%	5%	1%	0%
710239	Diamonds for jewelry worked but not mounted	2.1%	0%	0%	5%	5%	10%	0%
940540	Other electric lamps and lighting fittings[c]	1.5%	0%–25%	0%[d]	15%	15%	10%	0%
620213	Women's or girls' coats of artificial fibers, not knitted	1.2%	20%	0%	55%	55%	22%	0%
711319	Jewelry and parts of precious metals (excl. silver)	0.9%	25%	0%	14%	0%	20%	0%
620113	Men's or boys' coats of artificial fibers, not knitted	0.9%	20%	0%	55%	55%	22%	0%
Armenia's top 12 export products		76.1%						

Note: The cells for the products for which tariffs faced by Armenia's exports were actually reduced are highlighted.

EEU = Eurasian Economic Union, FTA = free trade agreement, HS = Harmonized System classification (1992 version), MFN = most-favored nation.

[a] The tariff rate quota applies to all EEU members, except the Russian Federation, which benefits from tariff-free access without limit. In 2017, Serbia imported $70 million of cigarettes and Armenia exported $231 million of cigarettes. In 2017, none of the four EEU countries subject to the tariff rate quota exported any cigarettes to Serbia. Assuming a $0.5 cost per pack, the tariff rate quota would allow the first $50 million of cigarettes to enter tariff-free, which suggests that the tariff rate quota will not be binding in the short- to medium-term.

[b] The tariff rate quota applies to all EEU members, except the Russian Federation (the FTA also excludes other hard liquors, which continue to be subject to the MFN tariff, except if they come from the Russian Federation, in which case the tariff is zero). The EEU does not export any cognac to Serbia. However, Serbia imported $4.6 million worth of cognac from other countries in 2017; and Armenia exported $1.4 million worth of cognac to Latvia in 2017, a country with a population 3.7 times lower and GDP 1.4 times lower than Serbia. This suggests an unrealized market potential for Armenia in Serbia. The tariff rate quota corresponds to 167,000 bottles of 75cl of 40° Cognac. Assuming a $5 cost per bottle, the tariff rate quota would only allow the first $0.8 million worth of cognac to enter tariff-free. This suggests that the tariff rate quota will not be binding in the short term, but that it could become so at some point.

[c] This category includes searchlights (94054020), other spotlights (94054040) lamps for lighting public space (94054050), exterior lighting (94054060), lamps for aerodromes, railway stock, locomotives and aircrafts (94054070), pilot lamps with fittings for electro-thermic domestic appliances (94054080), fiber-optic headband lamps for medical use (94054091), and other electric lamps and lighting fittings (94054099).

[d] For the seven HS 10-digit tariff lines for which tariffs are positive (5%–25%), tariffs were brought down to zero for 4 tariff lines in 2016, and gradually until 2020 for three other tariff lines.

Figure A1: Armenia's Imports in 2018 and Average Tariff Changes Occurring on 1 January 2021, by Sector

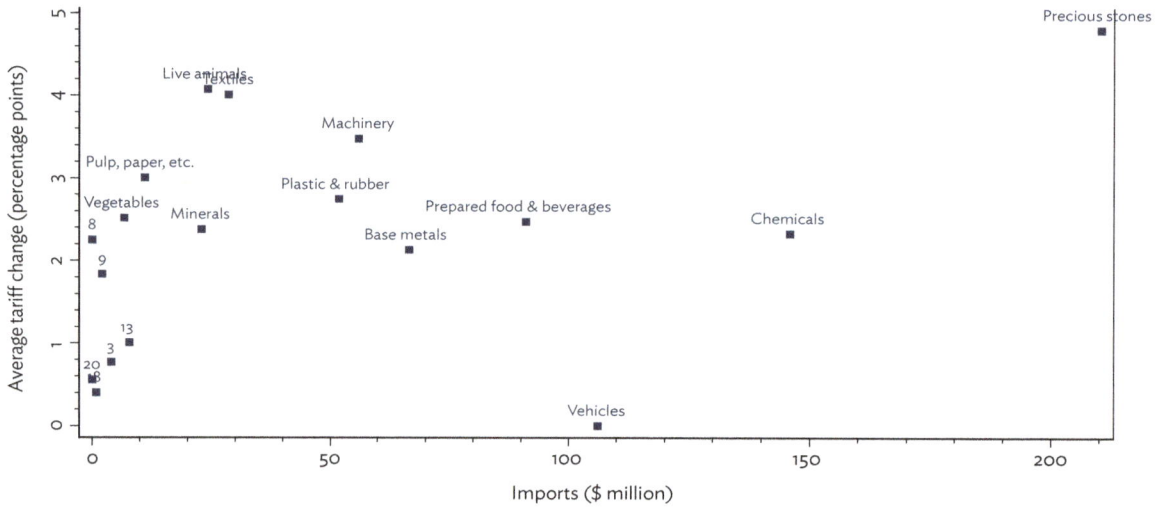

Note: Sectors correspond to sections in the Harmonized System (HS) classification (1992 version).
Sources: Asian Development Bank TA-9698 team calculation, based on Database for Analysis of International Trade (BACI) (Gaulier and Zignago, 2010) and tariff data from the Eurasian Economic Commission.

Figure A2: Armenia's Imports in 2018 and Average Tariff Changes Occurring on 1 January 2022, by Sector

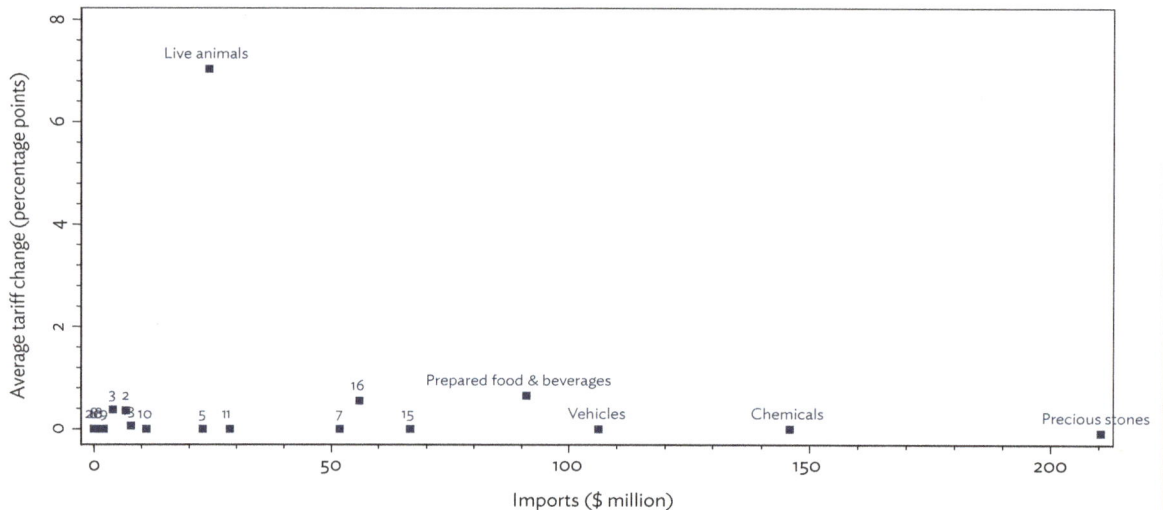

Note: Sectors correspond to sections in the Harmonized System (HS) classification (1992 version).
Sources: Asian Development Bank TA-9698 team calculation, based on Database for Analysis of International Trade (BACI) (Gaulier and Zignago, 2010) and tariff data from the Eurasian Economic Commission.

Figure A3: Distribution of Armenia's Tariffs in 2014, 2015, and 2022

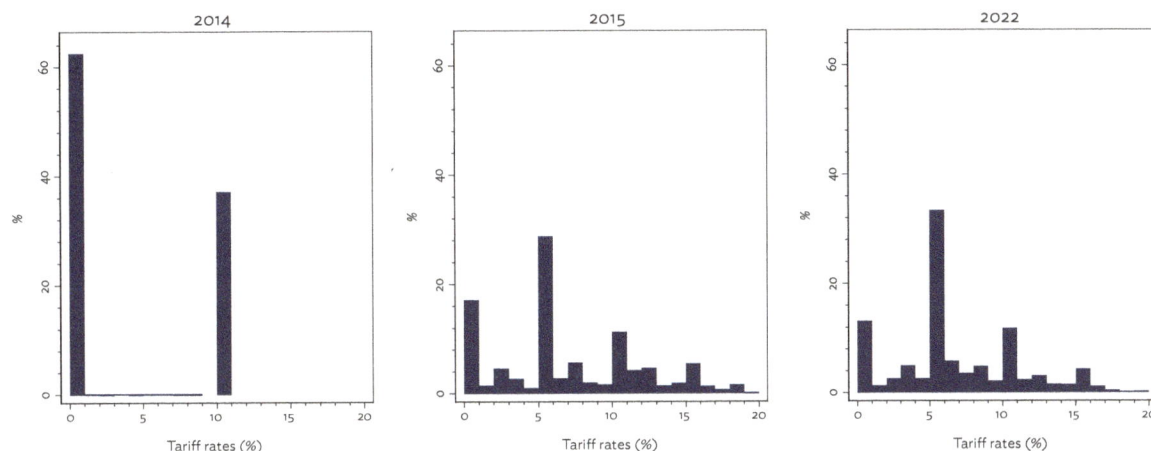

Note: To facilitate readability, distributions are truncated to exclude tariffs exceeding 20%.
Source: Asian Development Bank TA-9698 team calculations.

Table A4: List of 100 Economies with Comprehensive Bilateral Trade Coverage

AGO	ARE	ARG	ARM	AUS	AUT	AZE	BEL	BGD	BGR
BLR	BOL	BRA	CAN	CHE	CHL	CHN	CIV	COD	COL
CRI	CYP	CZE	DEU	DNK	DOM	DZA	ECU	EGY	ESP
EST	ETH	FIN	FRA	GBR	GEO	GHA	GRC	GTM	HKG
HRV	HUN	IDN	IND	IRL	IRN	IRQ	ISR	ITA	JOR
JPN	KAZ	KEN	KGZ	KOR	KWT	LBN	LKA	LTU	LVA
MAC	MAR	MDA	MEX	MLT	MMR	MYS	NGA	NLD	NOR
NZL	OMN	PAK	PAN	PER	PHL	POL	PRT	QAT	ROU
RUS	SAU	SGP	SRB	SVK	SVN	SWE	SYR	THA	TJK
TKM	TUR	TZA	UKR	URY	USA	UZB	VEN	VNM	ZAF

Note: Three-letter codes are from the ISO 3166 standard.

References

Anderson, J. and van Wincoop, E. 2003. Gravity with Gravitas: A Solution to the Border Puzzle. *American Economic Review.* 93(1): 170–92.

Arkolakis, C., Costinot, A., and Rodriguez-Claire, A. 2012. New Trade Models, Same Old Gains?. *American Economic Review.* 102(1): 94–130.

Asian Development Bank 2020. *Asia Regional Integration Center (ARIC)–Tracking Asian Integration.* Manila.

Bagdasarian, K. and Pakhomov, A. 2016. Issues Regarding Eurasian Economic Union Members' Participation in the WTO Activity. *Russian Economic Developments, Gaidar Institute for Economic Policy.* Vol. 11. 52–58.

Baier, S., Bergstrand, J. and Feng, M. 2014. Economic Integration Agreements and the Margins of International Trade. *Journal of International Economics.* 93(2): 339-350.

Baier, S., Yotov, Y. and Zylkin, T. 2019. On the Widely Differing Effects of Free Trade Agreements: Lessons from Twenty Years of Trade Integration. *Journal of International Economics.* Vol. 116. 206–226.

Eaton, J. and Kortum, S. 2002. Technology, Geography, and Trade. *Econometrica.* 70(5): 1741–1779.

Eurasian Economic Union (EEU) and Viet Nam. 2015. *Free Trade Agreement Between the Socialist Republic of Viet Nam, of the One Part, and the Eurasian Economic Union and its Member States, of the Other Part.* Burabay: Kazakhstan.

EEU and Serbia. 2019. *Free Trade Agreement Between the Eurasian Economic Union and its Member States, of the One Part, and the Republic of Serbia, of the Other Part.* Moscow: Russian Federation.

EU Commission. 2020. EU Regulation Amending Annexes II and III to Regulation (EU) No 978/2012 of the European Parliament and of the Council as regards Armenia and Vietnam. Brussels: Belgium.

Gaulier, G. and Zignago, S. 2010. BACI: International Trade Database at the Product-level – The 1994-2007 Version. *CEPII Working Paper* No. 2010-23.

Gnutzmann, H. and Gnutzmann-Mkrtchyan, A. 2019. The Cost of Borders: Evidence from the Eurasian Customs Union. *Hannover Economic Papers* N. 664, Leibniz Universität Hannover, Wirtschaftswissenschaftliche Fakultät.

Head, K. and Mayer, T. 2014. Gravity Equations: Workhorse, Toolkit, and Cookbook. *Handbook of International Economics.* Vol. 4. 131–195.

Head, K., Mayer, T. and Ries, T. 2010. The Erosion of Colonial Trade Linkages After Independence. *Journal of International Economics.* 81(1): 1–14.

Isakova, A., Koczan, Z. and Plekhanov, A. 2016. How Much do Tariffs Matter? Evidence from the Customs Union of Belarus, Kazakhstan and Russia. *Journal of Economic Policy Reform*. 19(2): 166–184.

International Trade Centre. 2020. Market Access Map (MacMap). Geneva: Switzerland.

Islamic Republic News Agency (IRNA). 2021. Iran to Permanently Join Eurasian Economic Union in Two Weeks: Parliament Speaker. Tehran: Iran.

Latypova, L. 2021. Iranian Speaker's Moscow Visit Signals Closer Ties to Come, Experts Say. *The Moscow Times*. Moscow: Russian Federation.

Olivero, M. and Yotov, Y. 2012. Dynamic Gravity: Endogenous Country Size and Asset Accumulation. *Canadian Journal of Economics*. 45(1): 64–92.

Ossa, R. 2015. Why Trade Matters After All. *Journal of International Economics*. Vol. 97. 266–277.

Santos Silva, J. and Tenreyro, S. 2006. The Log of Gravity. *The Review of Economics and Statistics*. Vol. 88. 641–658.

Simes, D. 2020. Russia Woos India to Sign Trade Pact with Eurasian Economic Union. *Nikkei Asia*. Tokyo: Japan.

Ter-Matevosyan, V., Drnoian, A., Mkrtchyan, N. and Yepremyan, T. 2017. Armenia in the Eurasian Economic Union: Reasons for Joining and its Consequences. *Eurasian Geography and Economics*. 58(3): 340–360.

Tinbergen, J. 1962. *Shaping the World Economy: Suggestions for an International Economic Policy*. The Twentieth Century Fund. New York, N.Y.: United States.

United Nations (UN). 2017. Harmonized Commodity Description and Coding Systems (HS). United Nations International Trade Statistics Knowledgebase.

United Nations Conference on Trade and Development (UNCTAD). 2021. Trade Analysis and Information System (TRAINS). Geneva: Switzerland.

Vinokurov, E. 2017. Eurasian Economic Union: Current State and Preliminary Results. *Russian Journal of Economics*. 3(1): 54–70.

Vinokurov, E., Demidenko, M., Korshunov, D., Pereboev, V., Tsukarev, T., Gubenko, R. and Khmarenko, E. 2017. *Eurasian Economic Integration – 2017*. Center for Integration Studies, Eurasian Development Bank. Report N. 43.

World Trade Organization (WTO) 2018a. *Factual Presentation: Treaty on Accession of the Republic of Armenia to the Eurasian Economic Union (Goods and Services)*. Report by the Secretariat. WT/REG363/1.

WTO. 2018b. *Factual Presentation: Treaty on the Eurasian Economic Union (Goods and Services)*. Report by the Secretariat. WT/REG358/1.

WTO. 2019. *Trade Policy Review: Armenia – 2018*. Report by the Secretariat. WT/TPR/S/379/Rev.1.

Yotov, Y., Piermartini, R., Monteiro, J. and Larch, M. 2016. *An Advanced Guide to Trade Policy Analysis: The Structural Gravity Model*. World Trade Organization. Geneva: Switzerland.